GARDEN BIRDS

How to attract birds to your garden

GARDEN BIRDS

How to attract birds to your garden

Dr. NOBLE PROCTOR

Consultant editors
Cyril Walker
Tim Parmenter

Rodale Press, Emmaus, Pennsylvania

A QUARTO BOOK

First published in Great Britain in 1985
Copyright © 1985 Quarto Publishing Limited

Published in 1986 in the United States of America by
Rodale Press, Inc.
33 East Minor Street
Emmaus, PA 18098

Distributed in the trade by
St. Martin's Press Inc.

Reprinted 1990

This book was designed and produced by
Quarto Publishing Limited
The Old Brewery
6 Blundell Street
London N7

Senior Editor: Stephen Paul
Editor: Liz Davies

Designer: Michelle Stamp & Alun Jones
Art Editor: Moira Clinch

Bird Artist: David Ord Kerr
Illustrators: Vana Haggerty, Norman Bancroft-Hunt
Chart Composition: Elly King

Art Director: Alastair Campbell
Editorial Director: Jim Miles

Library of Congress Cataloging in Publication Data
Proctor, Noble S.
    Garden Birds

    A Quarto Book
    Bibliography: P.
    Includes index
    1. Birds, Attracting of   2. Garden Fauna
I. Walker, Cyril.   II. Parmenter, Tim.   III. Title
QL676.5.P74 1986   639.9'78   85-24464
ISBN 0-87857-592-8
    4   6   8   10   9   7   5   hardcover

Typeset by Facsimile, Coggeshall, Essex
Color origination by Hong Kong Graphic Arts, Hong Kong
Printed by Lee Fung Asco Printers Ltd, Hong Kong

CONTENTS

INTRODUCTION

THERE MUST BE HUNDREDS of books about gardens and gardening. Inevitably, most of these deal with the layout of gardens from the aesthetic or purely practical point of view and, of course, contain a lot of information on garden plants of every shape and size. Since gardening is an important and valuable leisure pastime for millions of people, none of this is particularly surprising—but the average naturalist might be forgiven for gaining the impression that many gardening authors pay rather little attention to the abundant wildlife which shares the gardens. All too often, perhaps, the emphasis is on the artificial or contrived, to the neglect of the natural—it begins, possibly, with the simple division of plants into flowers and weeds, or with the classification of insects, animals and birds as pests or nuisances if they should dare to interfere with the tidy, controlled and regimented garden in any way.

Before all the gardeners who have read this far snarl in disagreement and throw the book into the trashcan, let it be said at once that the intention is not to decry formal or well cared-for gardens, nor to advocate wild, untidy and basically unmanaged plots—far from it. The suggestion is that it is perfectly possible to manage a garden for all the traditional reasons (and in most of the traditional ways) and at the same time make it good for birds. Space will not permit very much comment about other creatures, such as insects, mammals, reptiles and amphibians, nor will it allow more than a brief mention of weeds and wild flowers although you will find that these too often are compatible.

The motives behind maintaining a garden which you can share with birds could be debated almost endlessly, but the two main ones must involve the simple pleasure you derive from birds and a basic feeling that you are doing something to help them. The motives need be no more complicated than that.

The first part of the book is a guide to bird gardening. It considers the place of birds in the garden, the undoubted conservation value of gardens and habitat planning in the garden. This is followed by sections giving practical hints on the provision of water, what to plant and why, the safe use of garden chemicals, the problems of predators, bird feeding, and the provision of natural and artificial nest-sites.

Deciding what to include in this section, and indeed what to include in the rest of the book, has not been easy. It was first of all necessary to define what a garden means. The garden in the inner city is quite different from the garden in the countryside; some gardens adjoin the sea, or exist in mountain valleys, other are beside lakes and rivers and form clearings in forests and woods—an "average garden" is therefore rather difficult to define!

Nevertheless, an attempt has been made to envisage such a thing—the sort of garden situation known to most people—but the boundaries have been kept fairly elastic, so as to include large gardens, gardens with lakes, rivers or streams alongside, those adjoining woodland and farmland, and so on. The definition has also been broadened to include the immediate grounds of schools, hospitals, factories and business premises, but large parks and "estates" have been deliberately excluded. The list of 100 birds by no means includes all the species that visit gardens for example, some people have birds like black grouse, turnstones and snow buntings in their gardens quite regularly, but it covers those which are regular in many gardens and a small selection of "possibles" or more localized visitors.

A beautifully laid out water garden (left) which is pleasing to the eye, but is less than adequate for attracting many bird species. It is unsuitable because there are no gaps between the plants to allow a safe access to the water's edge.

This rock garden (above) suffers from the same problems as the water garden: there is no clear area which slopes to the water's edge. The large lily pads, however, will provide smaller species with a place from which to drink.

THE BIRD GARDEN

A BIRD GARDEN can bring a great deal of pleasure, pleasure in the sight of birds and in the feeling that you are doing something to help them, and there is no need to seek any further justification.

WHY A BIRD GARDEN?

PLEASURE BEGINS, perhaps, with the simple appreciation of color and all the marvelous ways in which plumage details vary. Some birds are immediately striking, like a warbler or any of the woodpeckers, while others are more subtly attractive, like thrushes and finches, or even (when you bother to look at them more closely) the more commonplace starlings and house sparrows. Then you begin to notice that birds move in many different ways: some hop, some run, others waddle. Some climb adroitly or, like chickadees, are accomplished acrobats. Some are very tame, even confident, while others are wary or unobtrusive. Once you have started to notice these things, you are already a bird watcher. The next step is to learn which bird is which and to find out more about their lifestyles.

You can study this in detail in the second section of the book where you will find descriptions of 100 species, but there is no "instant" way in which you can become an expert on bird identification. Learning your birds is a slow process of building up knowledge through experience, and a garden is one of the best possible places to start.

Note first the size—as big as a sparrow, smaller than a robin, and so on; then the general shape—slender like an oriole, perhaps, or plump like a towhee. Does the bird have a stout, seed-eater's bill, like a sparrow, or a fine, insect-eater's bill, like a warbler? How does it move? Does it run briskly and confidently, like a starling; hop in short spurts like a robin, or scratch about rather furtively like a thrasher? Once you have gained a general idea of the sort

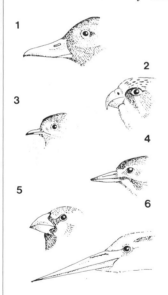

A bird's bill (above) indicates the type of food that it eats. Broad and flattened like a duck (1) for dabbling in mud and water to acquire plant and insect life. Hooked like a bird of prey (2) for tearing flesh. Needle-like; evolved for catching insects (3). Chisel-shaped (4) for prizing out grubs from behind the bark of trees. Short and deep (5) for crushing nuts and seeds. Dagger-like for spearing fish (6). A notebook (right) is a useful aid to help you remember the species spotted in the garden, especially when an unfamiliar or rare species requires detailed plumage description.

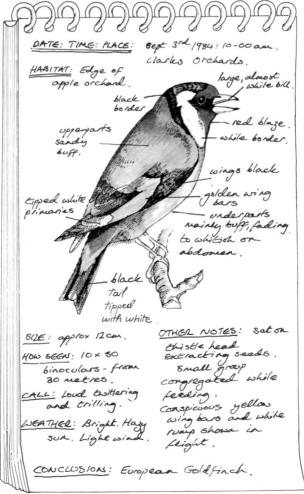

DATE: TIME: PLACE: Sept 3rd 1984: 10·00 am. Clarks Orchards.

HABITAT: Edge of apple orchard.

large, almost white bill.

black border

upperparts sandy buff.

red blaze

white border.

wings black

golden wing bars

underparts mainly buff, fading to whitish on abdomen.

tipped white primaries

black tail tipped with white

SIZE: approx 12 cm.

HOW SEEN: 10 × 50 binoculars - from 30 metres.

CALL: Loud twittering and trilling.

WEATHER: Bright. Hazy sun. Light wind.

OTHER NOTES: Sat on thistle head extracting seeds. Small group congregated while feeding. Conspicuous yellow wing bars and white rump shown in flight.

CONCLUSIONS: European Goldfinch.

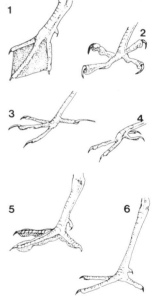

Like bills, birds' feet (above) are adapted for different uses. Fully webbed (1) for swimming. Short and powerful with long talons (2) for grasping or seizing prey. Three toes forward and one pointing backwards (3) for perching. Two toes forward and two backwards (4) for climbing. Palmated toes (5) to help swimming and walking on soft surfaces. Long-legged with a short hind toe (6) for walking on land.

of bird you are looking at, you can then move on to note the more obvious plumage features and the main areas of color.

Begin by looking at the whole upperparts, head and underparts; note particularly head and wing patterns, rump colors, whether or not the outer feathers in the tail are white—and so on. Once you have thoroughly mastered the most common visitors to the garden (and realized that even they might be tricky because of sexual differences, or seasonal plumages), finding that unusual or unexpected newcomer will be that much easier. You will also be much better equipped to start looking at birds away from the garden if, as often happens, bird gardening leads on to a wider interest in birds.

There is no doubt that feeding birds, providing them with water and, perhaps, nest-sites enhances your general enjoyment, especially since these often allow you to watch them at close quarters. But is there any substance in the feeling that you are also being useful to them?

Most bird gardeners can do little to offset the loss of some habitats which affects so many of the more specialized species, such as those of wetlands and heathlands. However, a positive contribution can be made towards the welfare of many woodland and woodland edge birds—birds of habitats which are fast disappearing in many areas. A carefully managed garden which caters for wildlife, especially if it can be designed to include plenty of trees and shrubs, is a positive asset. If you think of tens of thousands of sympathetically organized gardens as a great network of miniature nature reserves, your efforts begin to have real meaning—not just to you, but to the birds as well.

Feeding undoubtedly helps many small birds in winter, especially in very hard weather. In severe conditions it may become a significant factor in helping some vulnerable species to survive in reasonable numbers until

The mixed-foliage border of a well-designed garden (above) with an expanse of lawn in front. The large variety of plants provides numerous insects and cover for warblers and more skulking species; the trees and bushes behind offer a selection of breeding sites, and the lawn in front provides an open area on which other bird species can feed.

the following spring. Even if it is not, it is, of course, totally justifiable purely as a humanitarian response—and there is nothing wrong with that!

BIRD CONTROL AND THE LAW

GARDENS CAN MAKE an important contribution to wildlife conservation and it is perfectly possible to maintain a fairly normal, traditional garden and at the same time make it suitable for a variety of bird species. This is an important point in conservation—conserving wildlife is not merely a matter of putting a fence around something and not touching it at all. Habitats are dynamic and often change if left alone, so active management may be required just to preserve the status quo. As habitats change, so the bird, animal and insect communities within them change. Deciding to leave a garden entirely to nature could actually reduce its value to birds because you are reducing its diversity.

Managing your garden as a bird habitat is one thing—but should you take the management one step further and include the creatures living within the garden environment? There may be very sound gardening reasons for, say, the control of insect pests, carried out with no harmful side-effects to wildlife (see pages 28 to 31)—but control of garden pests is unlikely to benefit birds in any way at all. (Nor will it harm them if it is carried out properly.) What about the birds themselves? It is very tempting to think of some birds as "nice" and others as "nasty"—should some of these be controlled in any way? The answer is a firm NO (with the provision that you may, of course, wish to control some species because they are damaging fruit etc). Birds do not live as isolated entities, but as components in a mixed, interacting community, in effect, sharing the available resources and not, as a rule, competing directly with one another. Nature maintains the balance, and you can destroy it all too easily if you interfere; the birds can look after themselves within this balance of nature.

To some extent, your do produce an entirely artificial situation when your create feeding centers for birds. Perhaps the balance may seem to break down at this point, when it is clear that some birds hog the scene at the expense of others—feral pigeons, starlings and house sparrows especially. While in the strict sense that is natural and represents a normal and predictable shift in the balance, it is quite understandable that your should wish to step in and help . . . but the way to do this is by a system of gentle deterrents, and not by any attempt to control the species whose tactics you resent!

Any form of bird control—and this includes the control of pest species in the garden—is in any case subject to the

The destruction of crops (right) is a common problem. Rooks, pigeons and sparrows are among the main culprits, and the law stipulates that they may be "killed or taken by authorized persons at all times."

Feral pigeons can be a problem where food is readily available. They learn to visit likely sites regularly, and flocks may build up at places where a long-term and regular food supply is provided (left). This can be seen in city parks and squares where people enjoy feeding the birds. In smaller gardens this can become an embarrassment since they may crowd out the more timid species. The only way of avoiding the problem, should it arise, is to provide food in containers which do not permit the pigeons to reach it, but still allow the smaller and more agile birds access.

law, so it is as well to know what constraints the law applies. In the United States and Canada the legislation regarding bird control works on the important basic principle that all birds are protected. However, it does allow for certain exceptions — recognized pest species and certain birds which are accepted as quarry species for sporting purposes; but even then there are limitations on who can do what, and where, when and how.

In the United States Federal regulations prohibit the random extermination of any species, and contain general guidelines on bird control. These regulations have come about partly as a reaction to the persecution suffered by hawks and owls for many years. For a number of reasons these two species had gained the entirely unwarranted title of vermin and their numbers had been mercilessly depleted before the regulations came into force.

There are, however, some species that remain on a Federal listing as vermin, and these can, under certain circumstances, be removed. Redwing blackbirds, common grackles, magpies and starlings are some of the species that fall into this category, but even these are not open to "free-wheeling" extermination by unauthorized persons. In the United States a listing of vermin is held by every state's Department of Environmental Protection (DEP).

Apart from restrictions as to which may be controlled, there are further restrictions as to the locations where bird control may be practiced. A species listed as vermin may be taken by a landowner on his or her own land if it is seen an caught in the act of destruction. On other, private lands, permission must be gained from the landowner or someone acting with his or her permission to authorize the killing of any vermin species. The taking of waterfowl and game species is regulated by yearly hunting quotas. It should only be considered by persons with large areas of water and woodlands on their property. Indeed, landowners should take it on themselves to see that their property is clearly demarcated with posts so that the many species living or visiting their property are not subject to unlawful killing by unauthorized person.

THE ESSENTIALS: A BROAD OUTLINE

A BIRD GARDEN can exist in many forms, depending on its size and situation and, indeed, your own feelings on the subject. It could range from an almost wholly natural area to one which is intensively gardened in the traditional sense and yet is still good for wildlife. It is probably a mistake to think that a totally wild area is best for birds. Traditional gardening management is much more likely to produce a wider range of feeding opportunities than would normally occur in nature, especially through the planting of many varieties of plants and shrubs. A 50–50 compromise between "wild" and "tame" would be very suitable, but for most gardeners in most situations a mix of about 25/75 is perfectly adequate—in other words a normal, managed garden with provisions for wildlife.

The main factors to take into account are likely food plants; trees and shrubs for food, shelter, nest-sites and song-posts; the provision of water; where to put the winter feeding center; whether to provide artificial nest-

A patio garden situated in an urban area (above) can also be made suitable for birds. The only requirements are one or two bushy trees for nesting, a birdbath and a hanging feeder. Gardens located close to the coast will always produce a large number of species. In this instance (below) a freshwater pond and some low bushes would enhance the species' potential.

Small urban gardens, looked at individually, offer little for wildlife. However, a series of bushes in different plots (left) will provide a considerable amount of cover.

Access to water is often difficult for town birds. The provision of a simple bird bath (below) placed in an open area is a great help.

sites; and the one which is so often forgotten—how to arrange things so that you can actually *see* the birds from your windows. At an early stage too, careful thought should be given to whether there are some parts of the garden from which you wish to exclude birds at certain times of the year, for example, parts of the kitchen garden or particularly vulnerable fruit crops. You may have to accept that the simplest and most foolproof way of protecting these is by caging them in entirely with netting.

Most of what follows in this book is aimed at people with at least a reasonably-sized garden, so perhaps this is the place to say a few words about tiny gardens, places with no garden at all and the grounds of factories, hospitals, schools and so forth. Any sort of widescale bird gardening may be out of the question, but there is still quite a lot that can be done.

In many cases, those with no gardens can still feed the birds in winter and enjoy watching them. Bird tables and feeding trays which can be fixed to windowsills are available, and chickadee feeders to hang in windows or attach to the glass with a rubber sucker can easily be found. Flat-topped roofs may be adjacent to your windows and these can make excellent, king-size bird tables. With a little thought and not too much expense, they might even be worth planting up with a few tubs of berry-bearing shrubs for the winter. Even in big cities and in the middle of big factory complexes you will be surprised at how effective these relatively minor additions can be. There is no reason why nestboxes should not be put up on walls, as long as there are some gardens or areas with trees and shrubs not too far away where birds, like chickadees, can forage for the correct food for their young.

Business premises may have lawns or grassy banks or even a few flowerbeds. They are much improved by the planting of ornamental, berry-bearing shrubs like berberis and cotoneaster, or with trees such as flowering cherries, mountain ash and crab apple—all very attractive to the eye and all of value to birds. Wherever there are trees such as oaks, pines, birch and so on—in other words native species—these should be left in situ. School grounds often provide exactly the right opportunities for planting trees and shrubs, and, of course, for erecting bird tables and feeders, and here bird gardening can have an educational function too. Hospital grounds sometimes provide equally good opportunities— for example, where it is possible for patients to look out of windows, feeding stations can be set up, or nestboxes erected. Bird watching can, after all, be an excellent form of therapy.

Finally, some thought can be given as to whether such places might have an ornamental pond, or even a small lake—or, if not, a birdbath. Water is a sure attraction to many birds and is attractive on a formal lawn.

GARDENING FOR BIRDS

IN PLANNING TERMS, gardens fall into two categories—wholly new, untouched sites and existing gardens. The first type obviously provides a lot of scope and can be planned from scratch, whereas in the case of an established garden it is a question of taking stock of what is already there and thinking about how it might be changed or added to.

PLANNING THE GARDEN

BEFORE GOING ANY FURTHER, it is worth giving some thought to "wild areas", which can be provided in either sort of garden. Remember that even an area designated "wild" should not be an entirely neglected one—it will need a little management. It is usually best to maintain a wild area well away from your best flowerbeds and vegetable plots, simply to avoid the problem of weeds spreading to places where you do not want them. Choose a corner, or maintain a strip along a wall or fence where maintainance is easy and you can keep an eye on things. There is more about these areas later, but in passing note that plants like amaranth and lamb's quarters need little encouragement and should be retained to provide seeds for finches; thistles will attract goldfinches, as will teasels—which are also very attractive in their own right. Nettles may not be of much obvious use to birds, but they are invaluable to butterflies—if they can be left so that they grow close to or underneath buddleia, which attracts butterflies and a whole host of other insects, so much the better. Various grasses also provide seeds for small birds, but they also have a tendency to spread like wildfire and may need to be kept under control. Brambles too should be encouraged, perhaps in a corner of the garden or along a fence or wall. Birds enjoy blackberries just as much as humans and brambles can also provide nesting cover.

Starting from scratch

A new garden plot requires a lot of thought before it is planted. Look at the area around your garden and consider which birds are likely to come and what sort of conditions they would like. Think, too, whether there might be one or two local species which you might be able to attract by providing something special—a pond, perhaps, or a favorite food plant. Then draw up a plan, preferably on graph paper, taking into account the positions and likely eventual size of any existing trees and, of course, of other features such as clothes lines, garden sheds, greenhouses, fuel storage tanks and so on. Remember, too, to give early thought to any paths you may wish to lay out. Then plan where to put your flowerbeds, vegetable plots, shrubs and any trees you wish to plant, always bearing in mind lines of sight from

Trees such as this malus *(above) always provide excellent nesting sites for thrushes and finches. Fruits born by the tree, and insects attracted to it, are an important food source. Thistles (below) are attractive plants, which are pleasing to the eye. They will also coax more timid seed-eating birds into the garden.*

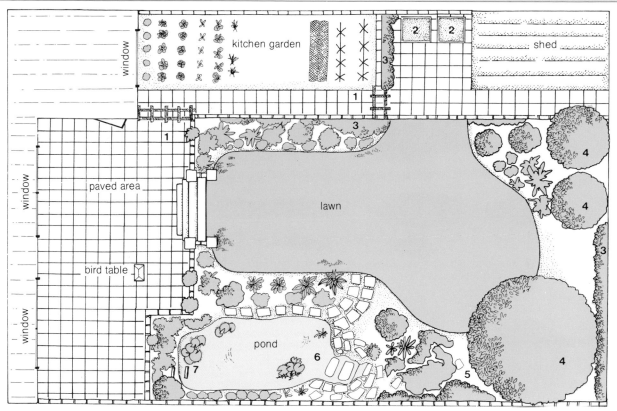

A suggested plan for an average garden, incorporating all the features which will attract birds (above). It may, of course, be adapted to suit the individual situation. Pergolas (1) for climbing plants, which will provide nest-sites. Compost heaps (2) attract insects and, therefore, provide a natural food source. Hedges (3) which bear fruit, such as cotoneaster, have a dual purpose: they are useful as nesting sites, and their berries provide food in the winter. Taller trees (4), especially evergreens, allow roosting and are excellent nest-sites. A wild (5) area will provide food, in the form of berries, and cover for skulking species. A pond (6) with open shallows allows easy access for drinking. Perches (7) distributed around the garden will encourage flycatchers.

Although this landscaped garden (left) provides very little for birds in the immediate foreground, the mature trees in the distance give ample cover and nesting sites for large species.

your windows so that you can actually see the birds which come. How much of the garden will be lawn? Don't be afraid to make your lawns a major feature and think in terms of planning the rest of the garden around them. Short grass maintained in the traditional way (but preferably with a little more tolerance than usual of clovers and buttercups) is used by a lot of birds.

Perhaps the most exciting possibility of all is to plan a garden pond. How big you make it, and what shape, will depend on the space available—but it will be a major attraction to birds and the insects on which many of them feed. If you are fairly close to larger water areas, streams, rivers or canals, think of the kingfisher as a likely visitor and provide both small fish and one or two suitable perches; remember too that ponds provide homes for frogs, toads and newts and also the chance to grow some interesting and very attractive plants.

Adapting the old

If you have a well-established garden (or are moving into a house which has one) and if, so far, little thought has been given to providing for birds, the first thing to do is to take stock of what is there and decide what should be retained, and where and how alterations might be made.

Large lakes with surrounding vegetation (right) will encourage many water birds such as ducks, swans, rails and herons. If the water level can be regulated so as to leave muddy margins, wader species may be tempted to rest and feed while on migration. Wet areas also harbour large numbers of insects which will attract swallows and other insect eaters.

The benefits of having a mature woodland (left) in a garden are enormous — many hole-nesting species, such as woodpeckers, creepers and chickadees, can find suitable cavities in which to breed and find food. It is important, however, that dead branches and trees (below) should be left, for they are important providers of nest-sites and food items.

On pages 20 to 27 you can see which plants, shrubs and trees to look for, or to add, but here is some general guidance about trees.

Trees

Mature trees are an asset in any garden, providing as they do song-posts, a variety of sources of natural food and many nesting-places. All too often there seems to be a tendency to regard them as a nuisance or potential source of danger, and to lop off big branches or even to think of felling. Obviously, where there is a distinct danger to houses, or if overhanging branches are a nuisance to neighbors and passers-by, some action is desirable—but try to keep tree control to a minimum and always seek professional advice first.

The other great temptation is to remove dead trees because they are unsightly, or to take off dead branches. In fact, dead wood often harbors a lot of insect food which is sought by woodpeckers, nuthatches, creepers and chickadees; it often provides opportunities for hole-nesters, like titmice, to breed and, above all perhaps, for woodpeckers to excavate nest-holes. Furthermore, dead limbs are used as drumming-posts by the hairy and downy woodpeckers in late winter and spring. So you should think twice before taking down dead wood—try to retain some of it if at all possible. It is, after all, a vital component of any woodland habitat and one which to some extent you can replicate in the garden.

ON THE WATERFRONT

IF YOU ARE LUCKY ENOUGH to move into a house with a river frontage, or a lake or decent-sized pond at the foot of the garden, spend some time watching what happens before planning any changes. Find out which waterside plants are growing there and which birds are using them for food or shelter. Large areas of reeds or so-called "bulrushes" may extend right across your frontage, and it is perhaps tempting to clear them away to give a clear view across areas of open water—but it may be much better to create a couple of large gaps in the cover, retaining some of it at either end and in a clump or two in the middle. This broken edge effect is likely to prove more attractive to more bird species than either a clear shoreline or a continuous, unbroken line of vegetation. By producing little bays and inlets you will provide loafing spots for duck, feeding areas for snipe and open crossing points which might help you to spot more furtive birds like the Virginia rail. You might also attract a heron and, if you provide one or two strategically placed perches, regular visits from a kingfisher.

If you are fortunate enough to have a long frontage on to a lake, it could pay dividends to think in terms of creating a length of irregular shoreline, with miniature bays, promontories and shallows. This will probably involve you in many hours' manual labor, but the chance of attracting more waterfowl and perhaps migrant waders like solitary and spotted sandpipers will make it very worthwhile. A big post in the water will also be useful as a perching place for a number of birds.

In upland areas, some gardens back on to rocky or fast-moving streams, where spotted sandpipers, and in the west, dippers, may all occur as breeding birds. Generally, it is not possible to manage the foot of your garden to attract these species, although a contrived bit of gravelly shore might help sandpipers and a garden pond should certainly attract green herons. If there is none in place already, it would be worth positioning a couple of large, round-topped stones in the water where you can see them. All these birds will find them and use them—dippers may pause to feed in the eddies around them.

One final point concerning water frontages: a relatively swift-moving lowland stream may provide you with the opportunity of growing your own cress if you have the room to divert the water across a shallow area. This leads not only to good eating, but produces excellent conditions for a number of birds, including pipits and even warblers.

In addition, shallow water areas may also serve to attract small numbers of hawks who relish shallow water in which they like to bathe.

Water for birds

Most people, of course do not have rivers, streams, lakes or ponds at the foot of their gardens, but for many bird gardeners the provision of water is often one of their first considerations. Birds need water to survive; you can provide it quite easily, either as a simple drinking or bathing supply, or in the form of a man-made pond.

Birdbaths are available in a variety of forms, either on pedestals or as precast or molded mini-pools for placing at ground level. All of these are perfectly acceptable to birds, but you can just as easily make your own, using an upturned trashcan lid or a small sheet of heavy gauge pond-liner. If you do make your own, remember to give the birds easy access from gently sloping sides, or via a brick or stone placed in the water. Remember that shallow water is all that is needed; keep it clean of leaves and debris and change the water regularly.

Water is important in winter and, even if you do not maintain a year-round supply for your birds, you should endeavor to provide it in hard weather. The problem is, of course, that water freezes easily—so what is to be done? *On no account* should you add any form of anti-freezing substance to the water: the chances are that it will do some harm to the birds. You can, of course, adopt the irksome course of going out and breaking the ice regularly, or adding warm water at intervals, but nowadays most people think instead of installing a simple heater to maintain the water temperature above freezing point. An aquarium heater, available at any good pet store, does the job perfectly well but it will, of course, require external, weatherproof wiring—a local electrician should be able to advise you on this aspect. If you are putting water out in a shallow container, for example a trashcan lid, it is very effective to raise the whole affair on bricks and place a simple nightlight in the space underneath it.

Making a pond

Making an artificial pond is an exciting prospect (at least, it is once you've dug the hole). This is in any case a popular and common practice among gardeners, and many of the better gardening books give excellent advice on what to do. A formal garden pool—even a fairly sophisticated water garden—will provide good conditions for birds, but in many ways a purpose-built pool is better. The only constraints are how much you want to spend and how much space you have available.

Broadly speaking, the aim is to produce a pond with a slightly irregular outline, shallow at the edges (or at least at one end) and not more that $3^1/_4$ ft deep in any place. It should provide "walk-in" access to birds and easily accessible drinking and bathing places. Through a mixture of native and more exotic plants, it can be both visually attractive and a good source of food for birds. A pool can be designed in conjunction with another garden

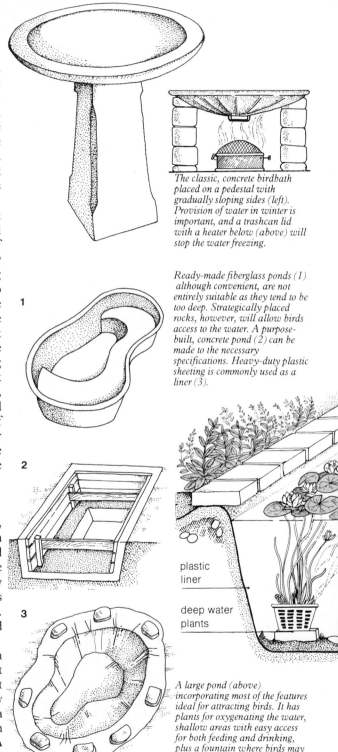

The classic, concrete birdbath placed on a pedestal with gradually sloping sides (left). Provision of water in winter is important, and a trashcan lid with a heater below (above) will stop the water freezing.

Ready-made fiberglass ponds (1) although convenient, are not entirely suitable as they tend to be too deep. Strategically placed rocks, however, will allow birds access to the water. A purpose-built, concrete pond (2) can be made to the necessary specifications. Heavy-duty plastic sheeting is commonly used as a liner (3).

1

2

3

plastic liner

deep water plants

A large pond (above) incorporating most of the features ideal for attracting birds. It has plants for oxygenating the water, shallow areas with easy access for both feeding and drinking, plus a fountain where birds may bathe.

feature—an adjacent rock garden perhaps. This could also provide a simple waterfall system whereby water is pumped up and returned to the pond by gravity, producing oxygenation which is essential for a successful and productive pond. The alternative is to stock the pool with plenty of oxygenating plants, hornwort, for example.

A heavy clay soil provides a ready-made pond-liner which will cost you nothing other than a lot of sweat and toil. But soils with good drainage require entirely artificial techniques for which there are three alternatives. It is possible nowadays to purchase quite large, molded glass fiber ponds which are excellent for the small garden. Their major disadvantage is that the size and shape is predetermined by the manufacturers. Preparing a concrete lining, and coating it with plastic paint, gives you much greater flexibility, but is laborious and, once completed, very difficult to alter in any significant way. A better alternative is to line your excavation with heavy-duty plastic sheeting, which is no more expensive than the other methods and is much more flexible in design terms.

At all stages of construction, extreme care must be taken not to damage or puncture the sheeting. It is important to provide a reasonably smooth base on which to lay the sheeting and then to lay it generously, to allow for its movement and settling when soil is placed upon it, and again when you add the weight of the water. Allow a wide overlap at the edges and do not trim off the surplus until the whole pond is completed and filled. Again, be

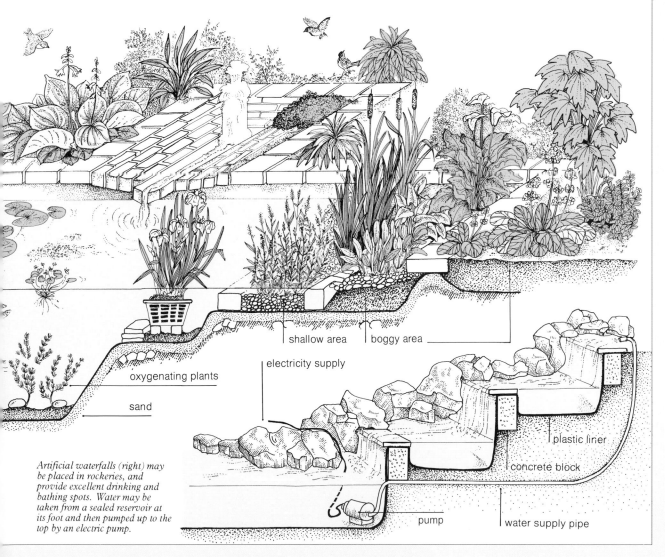

shallow area   boggy area

electricity supply

oxygenating plants

sand

plastic liner

concrete block

Artificial waterfalls (right) may be placed in rockeries, and provide excellent drinking and bathing spots. Water may be taken from a sealed reservoir at its foot and then pumped up to the top by an electric pump.

pump   water supply pipe

very careful not to damage the sheeting if any large stones, plant containers etc are to rest on it.

Rainwater would eventually fill your pool, but it is better and faster to do it from the tap, using a hose pipe. Add a few buckets of water from a local pond to help introduce the first micro-organisms to the new environment. Allow the water to settle for about two weeks (topping up the level if necessary) before any planting is undertaken. The layer of soil you have placed on the pond-liner will provide most of what you need for planting, but plants in containers can also be placed as required; use some of the soil from the excavation to build up a low surround to incorporate the overlap of the sheeting and to provide a good moisture-retaining base for waterside plants.

Stocking the pond

Many of the plants available commercially for garden ponds will be suitable, but, for a more natural look, a much better strategy is to introduce a majority of native species—the sort of things that grow in real ponds in your area. However, the law places certain restraints on the uprooting of wild plants, even common ones. Be sure that you have the necessary permission before going to your local pond for supplies; take only a few plants of the kinds you need and cause as little damage as possible while doing so. Choose only places where these plants are abundant. In many ways, it is often better to scrounge what you want from neighbors or friends with established ponds. As already mentioned, hornwort is an excellent oxygenating plant. Some other useful species you can

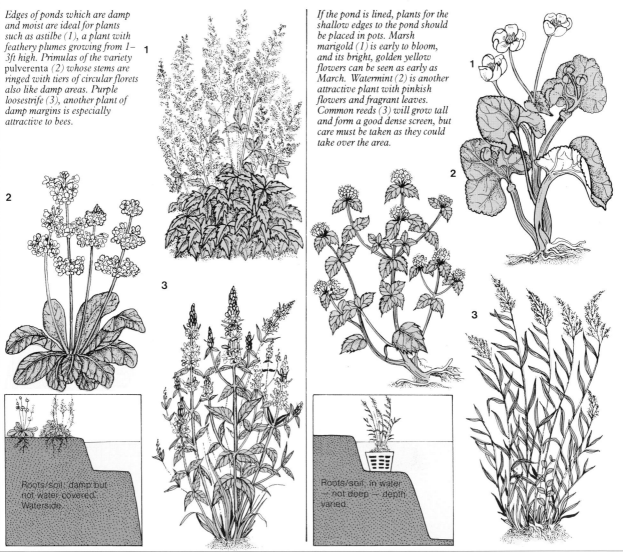

Edges of ponds which are damp and moist are ideal for plants such as astilbe (1), a plant with feathery plumes growing from 1–3ft high. Primulas of the variety pulverenta *(2) whose stems are ringed with tiers of circular florets also like damp areas. Purple loosestrife (3), another plant of damp margins is especially attractive to bees.*

If the pond is lined, plants for the shallow edges to the pond should be placed in pots. Marsh marigold (1) is early to bloom, and its bright, golden yellow flowers can be seen as early as March. Watermint (2) is another attractive plant with pinkish flowers and fragrant leaves. Common reeds (3) will grow tall and form a good dense screen, but care must be taken as they could take over the area.

Roots/soil: damp but not water covered. Waterside.

Roots/soil: in water — not deep — depth varied.

introduce include water mint, water forgetmenot, water plantain, marsh marigold, marestail, yellow or blue flag iris, bogbean, purple loosestrife, frogbit (floating), amphibious bistort (floating) and (at the deepest parts) water lilies. Cat-tail *(typha)* will grow well around the wet edges, as will bog arum, primulas and various ferns. The cat-tails will form big, attractive stands and may need some control as your pond matures; unless you have a lot of room or are prepared to carry out continuous management it is probably not a good idea to introduce the highly invasive and fast-spreading common reed *(phragmites)*.

There is a good chance that the American toad (and perhaps newts) will colonize unaided—but here, too, you can ask a friend or neighbor for spawn or tadpoles from a well-established pond. A supply of the spawn of the American frog could be even more valuable. This has become a scarce animal in some areas, and founding a new, protected colony could be an important local conservation project. Remember that both frogs and toads require easy access into and out of the pond—gently sloping banks or strategically placed stones will help them. They also like flat stones placed in the water, both at and just under the surface. During hot weather watch for falling water levels and adjust the exits accordingly.

Bird gardeners will welcome visits by kingfishers and green herons, but the latter can be unpopular in gardens where ponds are stocked with goldfish and other ornamental species. Netting over the water is an effective way to stop predation, while erecting simple string or wire

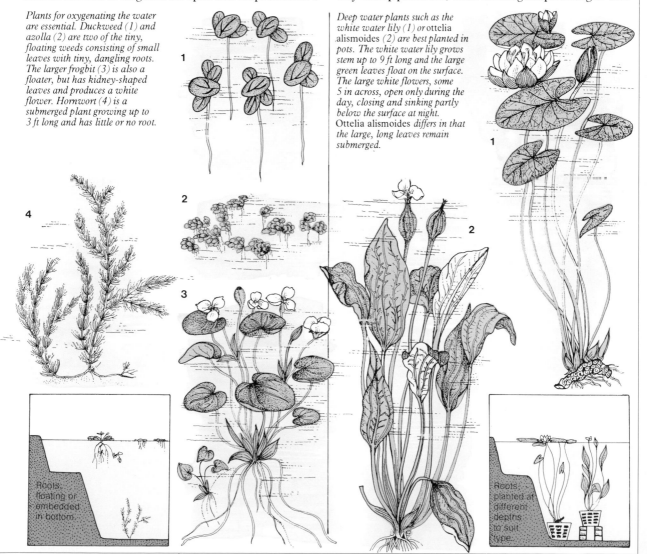

Plants for oxygenating the water are essential. Duckweed (1) and azolla (2) are two of the tiny, floating weeds consisting of small leaves with tiny, dangling roots. The larger frogbit (3) is also a floater, but has kidney-shaped leaves and produces a white flower. Hornwort (4) is a submerged plant growing up to 3 ft long and has little or no root.

Deep water plants such as the white water lily (1) or ottelia alismoides *(2) are best planted in pots. The white water lily grows stem up to 9 ft long and the large green leaves float on the surface. The large white flowers, some 5 in across, open only during the day, closing and sinking partly below the surface at night.* Ottelia alismoides *differs in that the large, long leaves remain submerged.*

Roots: floating or embedded in bottom.

Roots: planted at different depths to suit type.

21

lines around the edges of the pool can also be an effective deterrent. Model herons or heron-like birds often make bird gardeners groan with distaste, but they, too, can prove quite effective deterrents in the short term. Fortunately, green heron predation tends to be rather seasonal, at least at garden ponds, usually involving mainly young birds in late summer and fall.

TREES AND SHRUBS

TREES PROVIDE BIRDS with song-posts, roost-sites, nesting-places and food, either directly through their seeds, nuts or fruits, or indirectly through the insects they attract. Anything with reasonably thick foliage might provide a roost-site; ornamental evergreens are best for this, but beyond planting a few of these there is not much you can do. The shrubs described later are often better. Similarly, you should not worry too much about providing song-posts; most birds will use whatever is available, including roofs, television aerials, wires, as well as trees and bushes.

Trees
As far as possible, existing trees—especially native or long-established kinds—should be retained. Ideally, too, you should not be in too much of a hurry to remove dead

The beech (left) with its seed, the "mast", falling in fall will attract many types of finch; it is also favored by chickadees, nuthatches and woodpeckers.

The alder (right) is a favorite of the siskin, especially when planted in damp areas. Redpolls also feed on the seeds in the tiny cones and warblers thrive on the insects.

Mountain ash (left) with its crop of bright red berries is a colorful addition to any garden. Wood thrushes are very partial to the fruit as well as other thrushes and blackbirds.

The oak (above) is probably host to more species of insect than any other tree, thus supplying food for many bird species; pigeons and jays feed on the acorns.

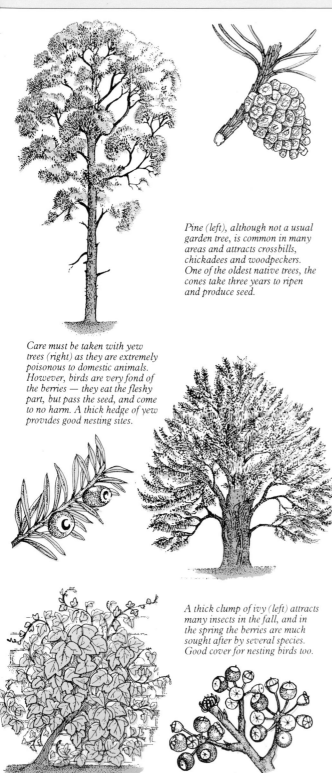

Pine (left), although not a usual garden tree, is common in many areas and attracts crossbills, chickadees and woodpeckers. One of the oldest native trees, the cones take three years to ripen and produce seed.

Care must be taken with yew trees (right) as they are extremely poisonous to domestic animals. However, birds are very fond of the berries — they eat the fleshy part, but pass the seed, and come to no harm. A thick hedge of yew provides good nesting sites.

A thick clump of ivy (left) attracts many insects in the fall, and in the spring the berries are much sought after by several species. Good cover for nesting birds too.

wood as this can often provide useful insect food and potential nest-holes for several species. If you have enough room, elm is a thoroughly worthwhile tree and even one with Dutch elm disease, though unsightly, will be of benefit to birds for several years after its infection and death. If it is safe, think about retaining it for a time.

Trees to retain and trees to plant can be dealt with together. Important considerations in both cases are preferred soil type, eventual height and size and the likely spread of the tree—and whether it is safe to have it close to the house. Remember, too, that many trees are relatively slow-growing and will not reach maturity for a long time. Big trees really belong in big gardens. For most people, smaller species have to do instead—but many of these are of equal value to birds.

Small ornamental conifers and maples, while very popular, are of limited value to birds, except that they provide some cover and nest-sites. Most are of little value for food. Native or well-established species are far better. Oaks are used by approximately 300 species of insects, and they also provide valuable nest-sites and, of course, grow the acorns which are much appreciated by wood ducks and jays. Willows are also immensely rich in insect life, with some 250 insect species recorded and a useful supply of seeds in the fall. As with oaks, some of the ornamental varieties are almost as good as the native kinds.

Poplars may have up to 100 insect species on them, birch can have as many as 225 species and its catkins provide good spring feeding for redpolls and many other small birds.

Beech trees provide nuts in fall — the popular beechmast which is eagerly sought after by, among others, grouse, wood ducks and wintering evening grosbeaks.

Ash is another useful tree: pine grosbeaks are particularly fond of ash-keys. The rowan or mountain ash would be a beautiful tree to introduce into a garden situation even if its berries attracted no birds at all — but thrushes and waxwings love them!

Cherry trees of various kinds, crab apples and several ornamental trees produce fruits which are attractive to birds, especially thrushes, sometimes rose-breasted grosbeaks and, in the occasional winters when they appear in large numbers, Bohemian waxwings. Holly provides excellent cover, roosting and nesting places and berries. Gardeners (unless they are also avid wine-makers) tend to look askance at elderberry, but it is a good berry-bearing and insect-rich species, favoured by many small birds in fall especially. Hazel, too, is a good tree for its cover and its nuts. There are, in fact, many more useful trees in the broadleaf group: shadbush, Eleagnus, chokecherry and privet, for instance. Special mention should also be made of alder, which likes wet or very damp places and is a likely species alongside rivers or lakes. It is another very rich "bird tree", popular with chickadees, warblers, creepers and, especially, redpolls and siskins.

Of the conifers, yew is one of the best, providing thick cover and berries which, while they are harmful to man and domestic animals, are eaten by many birds like thrushes and greenfinches. Chickadees, bushtits and titmice feed on the insects in yews and also in pines. This handsome tree (and several of its close relatives) produces cones which also attract crossbills.

Both the European and the Japanese larches are similarly excellent trees for birds — and so, in fact, are many of the larger more exotic conifers widely planted in bigger gardens, such as cedars and even, in really big gardens, the majestic redwoods.

Fruit trees must be mentioned. Apples in particular are a favorite of many birds, such as thrushes and waxwings. Rose-breasted grosbeaks may damage the buds in spring, of course, making them unpopular with gardeners at that time. If you can, leave a few apples on the trees for the birds, and some windfalls on the ground.

At this point, some mention must be made of ivy, which grows both on trees and on houses. It actually does little harm to trees, despite popular opinion, and can be kept within reasonable bounds on walls. Few plants are as good for birds: ivy provides cover, nest-sites for many species (such as house finches and cardinals), a rich variety of insect food and a late and welcome supply of berries from January to March.

Shrubs

Many of the general observations made about trees apply also to shrubs. Again, soil requirements, size, spread and so forth have to be taken into account. Many of the larger, denser species provide potential nest-sites and some of the very large kinds, if planted in groups, may also provide cover for winter roots. At first sight, a mass of rhododendrons might seem useful, but, while birds roost and occasionally nest in them they generally provide little insect life or food and allow precious little to grow in their dense shade. Attractive though they are, while in flower, there are many better choices for the bird garden.

A wild, natural hedge, with hawthorns, perhaps blackthorn, wild roses, brambles, the odd small tree and all the many plants associated with such a habitat will be immensely rich in food for birds. Such things are well worth preserving, or even creating if at all possible. For many gardeners this is not a realistic proposition and they will have to think instead of a more formal hedge. If so, privet is very good; so is holly and, while it is slow-

growing, a yew hedge is probably even better still.

Rose bushes, especially climbers, are good for insects and their fruits. Honeysuckle, too, provides succulent berries and masses of insect food, as well as good nesting places; firethorn is attractive in a different way but every bit as good. There are many shrubs which you can plant for their berries, such as several kinds of berberis, snowberry, guelder rose and of course cotoneaster, especially *c simonsii* and *c x watereri. Cotoneaster horizontalis* grows over and along walls and is the waxwing shrub par excellence. Other attractive shrubs of

Several garden varieties of hawthorn (above) are available and these can make an excellent hedge for birds to nest in. The red berries are much favored by blackbirds.

Try to be sure to get a female holly tree (below) as only these produce the red berries which attract thrushes. The holly also makes a good hedge.

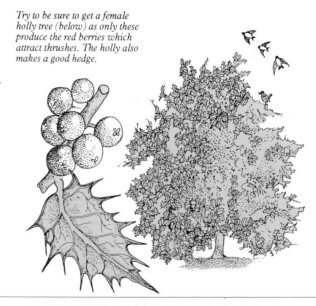

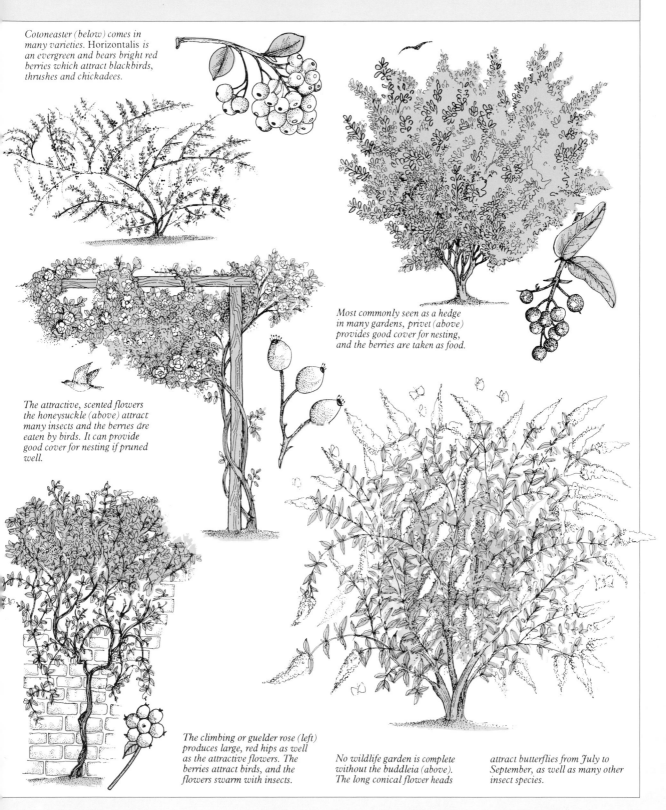

Cotoneaster (below) comes in many varieties. Horizontalis is an evergreen and bears bright red berries which attract blackbirds, thrushes and chickadees.

Most commonly seen as a hedge in many gardens, privet (above) provides good cover for nesting, and the berries are taken as food.

The attractive, scented flowers the honeysuckle (above) attract many insects and the berries are eaten by birds. It can provide good cover for nesting if pruned well.

The climbing or guelder rose (left) produces large, red hips as well as the attractive flowers. The berries attract birds, and the flowers swarm with insects.

No wildlife garden is complete without the buddleia (above). The long conical flower heads

attract butterflies from July to September, as well as many other insect species.

good value to wildlife include dogwood, Japanese quince and Russian olive.

Finally, there is buddleia, often called the "butterfly bush." Its principal attraction is indeed for butterflies, which may come in vast numbers, and for this reason alone it is a must in any wildlife garden—but it attracts masses of other insects too and so is used by many birds in late summer and fall.

FLOWERS AND WEEDS

A GARDEN WHICH IS RICH in flowering plants is generally also one which is rich in insects and, therefore, one which will attract a good many birds. To this extent, the more traditional idea of gardening is already valuable to wildlife. Flowerbeds which incorporate a good mixture of classic garden plants and shrubs form ideal mini-habitats, especially when the flowers chosen also provide seeds for birds. Well-vegetated banks covered with lesser periwinkle, or possibly large periwinkles, form excellent alternative borders, rich in insect life and also provide cover for voles (which are generally not regarded as

significant garden pests).

Good all-round plants for birds include forgetmenots, cornflowers, cosmos, asters, scabious, evening primrose and antirrhinums; many ornamental thistles and grasses are good for seeds, and may be easier to control than their wild counterparts. Sunflowers are a must in a good bird garden, not only for their seeds, but also for the many insects they attract. The list of worthwhile plants is actually a very long one—a shortened version would include michaelmas daisy, hebe, iceplant, petunia, sweet rocket, night-scented stock, valerian, pink, thyme, primrose, godetia, lobelia, candytuft, clarkia, mignonette, balsam, marjoram, honesty, aubretia, lavender, foxglove, larkspur and wallflower.

The sort of flowerbeds which are the best of all for birds and other wildlife are, unfortunately, the kind which are anathema to most gardeners—ones where weeds (or to be more fair to them, wildflowers) are allowed to co-exist with garden plants. A half-managed or "lazy gardener's" flowerbed is ideal in many ways, but in the interests of common sense it would be wrong to recommend letting the weeds run riot and take over altogether; this would in

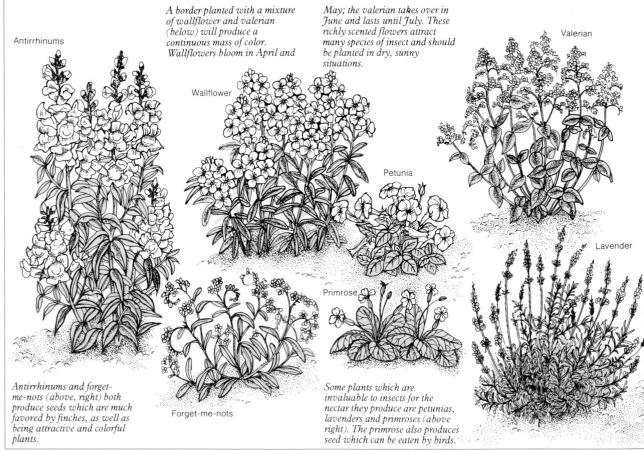

A border planted with a mixture of wallflower and valerian (below) will produce a continuous mass of color. Wallflowers bloom in April and May; the valerian takes over in June and lasts until July. These richly scented flowers attract many species of insect and should be planted in dry, sunny situations.

Antirrhinums

Wallflower

Valerian

Petunia

Lavender

Primrose

Antirrhinums and forget-me-nots (above, right) both produce seeds which are much favored by finches, as well as being attractive and colorful plants.

Forget-me-nots

Some plants which are invaluable to insects for the nectar they produce are petunias, lavenders and primroses (above right). The primrose also produces seed which can be eaten by birds.

Sunflowers (left) are not only attractive, but if left to seed they provide invaluable food for finches and chickadees. The seeds can also be collected for putting out on the bird table in the winter.

any case ruin the habitat. Totally bare soil between garden plants is unnatural, but is an accepted ideal in the garden—a good compromise is a flowerbed with garden plants and some wildflowers and some bare soil between them; this seems to be the mixture birds like best of all.

Many bird gardeners try to set aside a strip or a corner which is, effectively, a weed garden in which wild plants are allowed to grow, with some control and, of course, some consideration of the views of the neighbors. Wild grasses are a problem because they are highly invasive and spread like wildfire. They can be contained if you have a reasonably large garden and if you expend a lot of energy on occasions, but are perhaps best avoided in small gardens. Nettles, too, need control, but a space should be set aside for a nettle-patch, if at all possible. Their main value is to several species which lay their eggs on nettles and whose caterpillars then feed on the leaves, but birds can of course benefit from the caterpillars. One of the most useful things to do for a good butterfly garden is to plant nettles in close proximity to buddleia. Thistles (which may need careful control) and teasels are attractive in their own right and also attract goldfinches

Poppies (below) will brighten up any garden with their bright red flowers, and the seeds produced are attractive to finches.

Thistles (below), if left to seed, are a favorite of goldfinches, while the nettle is an invaluable food plant.

Dandelion

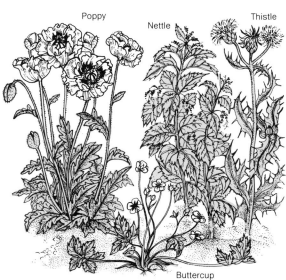

Poppy

Nettle

Thistle

Buttercup

Dandelions and buttercups (left, above) generally thought of as weeds, are nevertheless colorful plants and attract many species of insect. Dandelion seeds are also eaten. Care must be taken that these do not spread too much and take over the garden.

to their seeds. Poppies provide seed for birds (note that there are also several useful cultivated varieties which may be just as good). Other valuable weeds which produce seed for wild birds include some which are traditionally uprooted whenever they show up in most gardens—docks, sorrel, ragwort, groundsel and dandelions. Many umbellifers are also rich in insects, but beware the huge and spectacular giant hogweed which is now naturalized in many places. It is a menace to humans because it can cause a painful and very unpleasant skin rash and is best avoided altogether.

Finally, a traditional, mown lawn is very good for birds; it is even better if you allow clovers, buttercups and dandelions to grow in it. Blackbirds, thrushes, robins, starlings and many others find a rich supply of invertebrate food on lawns. Long, unmown grass is distinctly less useful to most birds, but could be maintained in small clumps or at the edges of a lawn in larger gardens.

CONTROL METHODS

THERE ARE A GREAT MANY CHEMICALS available to the gardener for use in pest control; the bird gardener should see that they are not harmful to wildlife.

Slugs
Frequent garden pests, they can be caught and destroyed by simple traps—a shallow, but steep-sided container sunk in the ground and filled with a sweet liquid works very well; so does a hollowed-out half orange placed open side downward. Chemical slug killers contain *metaldehyde* and *nuthiocarb*, both of which can harm

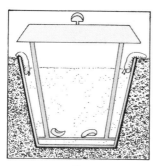
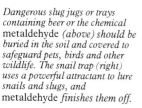

Dangerous slug jugs or trays containing beer or the chemical metaldehyde *(above) should be buried in the soil and covered to safeguard pets, birds and other wildlife. The snail trap (right) uses a powerful attractant to lure snails and slugs, and* metaldehyde *finishes them off.*

CONTROLLING PESTS IN THE GARDEN

Weeds in the Garden
There are several ways to eliminate weeds from the garden without using chemical herbicides. Remember, too, that some weeds (groundsel, thistle and dock, for example) are beneficial to birds.

Fertilization: Declining soil fertility is one cause of weed growth. Many types of weeds appear to thrive only on soil that is low in some minerals and has an excess of others. Building up a soil organically, and providing well balanced mineral fertilization, is one of the best ways to minimize weed problems.

Cultivation: In some gardens, particularly large ones, cultivation is necessary to keep weed growth to a minimum. A soil rich in organic matter is easily worked, and its cultivation and tillage can be timed advantageously to keep weed growth down.

Mulching: Mulching is another way to eliminate weeds from the garden. Straw, leaves and other organic matter can be piled thickly between rows and between plants in rows and beds. A thick mulch will suppress weed growth, but even if weeds emerge they can be controlled by piling more mulch on them.

Biological controls: The planned introduction of insects and fungus organisms that destroy weeds is a relatively new and promising development. Biological control of weeds is most useful when one kind of weed is overrunning an area. Biological weed controls are commercially available.

Weeds in the Lawn
Factors that can contribute to lawn weeds include insect damage, disease, and overwatering.

Fertilization: A dense turf is probably the best all-around weed control measure. Grass is very aggressive when fertilized generously. If weeds trouble your lawn, increase the use of fertilizer.

Preventing seed set: The secret of controlling annual lawn weeds, such as crabgrass, is to prevent them from developing seeds. If you prevent seed set for several seasons and simultaneously develop dense turf, crabgrass and other annual weeds should cease to be a problem.

Hand weeding: If your lawn is not too large, hand weeding can prove very effective. It may be a big job at first, but using fertilizer in conjunction with weeding will thicken the turf and greatly reduce the amount of weeding required next season.

Insects

Beneficial insects, such as bees and ladybugs, are welcome inhabitants of the garden and landscape. Insect pests can be controlled or eliminated with a variety of organic treatments, as described below.

Ants: Ants feed on "honeydew" excreted by aphids. Control of aphids will generally eliminate ants.

Aphids: Spray infested foliage with soapy water, then rinse with clear water. Use rotenone for severe infestations. For fruit trees, use dormant-oil spray in early spring.

Bean Beetles: Handpick. For heavy infestations apply rotenone or pyrethrum.

Flea Beetles: Dust with diatomaceous earth or rotenone for serious infestations.

Japanese Beetles: Dust with milky spore disease to control grubs, rotenone for adults.

Brown Stink Bugs: Weed control is best preventive measure.

Harlequin Bugs: Apply pyrethrum or sabadilla for serious infestations.

Tarnished Plant Bugs: Apply sabadilla for serious infestations.

Caterpillars: Handpick. Use *Bacillus thuringiensis* for serious infestations.

Carrot Rust Fly: Sprinkle rock phosphate around base of plants.

Leaf Miners: Remove and destroy infested leaves.

Mealybugs: Spray foliage with soapy water.

Scales: Spray fruit with dormant-oil spray in early spring.

Whiteflies: Dust with tobacco dust or apply insecticidal soap.

Diseases

The best treatment for plant disease is prevention, sanitation and the use of resistant varieties. Keep the garden and lawn free of weeds and debris, and try to provide optimum environmental conditions for plant growth. Waterlogged soil and poor air circulation among plants are two conditions that invite disease. When disease does strike, remove and destroy the infected plants immediately. Rotating crops can help keep susceptible plants out of infected areas where disease organisms may be harbored. Bacteria and other organisms can lie in the soil for years.

Bacterial Diseases: Often can be identified by symptoms. Rots cause leaves, stems, branches and tubers to become soft, slimy and ill-smelling. Wilting not caused by drought is another symptom of bacterial attack. Galls result from an overgrowth of cells in the plant. Bacterial wilt pathogens are encouraged by too much nitrogen in the soil. Best strategies for control include use of disease-free seed and resistant varieties, and crop rotation. Remove and destroy immediately any wilted plants.

Fungal Diseases: Mildews appear as pale powdery patches on leaves. Leaf spot fungi cause round, yellow to yellow-green spots that darken with time. Gray mold causes grayish, downy patches on fruits, flowers or vegetables. Damping-off causes stems of young seedlings to wither and collapse. Fungal diseases are often treated with various chemical sprays and dusts. But organic gardeners can safely rely on sanitation, removal of diseased plants, and use of resistant varieties.

Viral Diseases: Can invade all parts of a plant. Spread by insects, contact with tools and gardeners' hands, propagating from infecting plants, planting in infected soil. Typical symptoms include small yields of poor quality, and sometimes, rapid death. Mosaic produces yellow and green mottling and spotting of leaves. Another group of viruses causes yellowing, leaf curling, dwarfing or excessive branching. Eliminate infected plants immediately, and try to control spread of virus by means described above.

wildlife and pets. Do not sprinkle such baits in the open, but be sure to place them under a board, brick or flowerpot where birds and hedgehogs cannot reach them—or the poisoned slugs.

It is also worth mentioning that the compounds used in the treatment of roof timbers will kill bats. If you have bats in your roof but need to treat your timbers, consult an expert through the organizations listed on page 156.

Rodent control

The control of rodents may be necessary in some circumstances. Where mice are eating fruit or bulbs stored indoors, a standard breakback trap is ideal, but must not be used outdoors. If rodenticides are used where voles or mice are eating garden plants, they should always be placed in a covered situation where birds cannot get at them. The same applies to rat poison, which should be placed in a pipe or inside a pile of bricks and stones.

Birds

Birds are often best kept off vulnerable fruits by netting, or other types of covers. Other safe bird

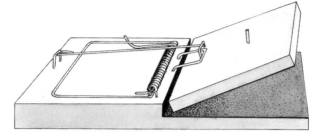

Where mice are a pest to crops or stored vegetables, the simple backbreaking trap (below) is not to be recommended for outdoor use, as birds are just as likely to get caught.

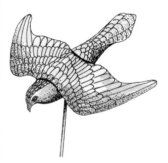

To discourage birds from eating fruit crops, a plastic kestrel mounted on a flexible pole (left) which moves in the wind, or an enclosed fruit cage is the best solution. The cage (below) consists of small mesh netting supported on a frame of metal poles. Care must be taken that no gaps are left — birds will find their way in through them, but then may not be able to escape so that you may have to dismantle part of the cage to let them out.

Although insect pests are not desirable, if you want to have a complete avifauna in your garden you have to accept that some insect damage is inevitable. If the damage to fruit-bearing plants becomes, or achieves, plague proportions you may wish to resort to pesticides. It must be remembered, however, that all pesticides are poisonous and must be used sparingly, for they are not only toxic to birdlife but can also be dangerous to pets and even humans. It is best to spray (left) on days when there is no wind, so that you prevent the materials spreading over a wide area, and causing unnecessary mortalities (above).

repellants include tin can lids, strips of aluminum foil or shredded plastic bags strung along a length of twine or wire and suspended between two stakes in the garden.

Safe use

All garden pesticides are poisonous, even botanical insecticides. If you do use botanicals, such as *rotenone* or *pyrethrum*, use them only as a last resort, and bear the following points in mind.

Do not buy any pesticide which does not include details of its ingredients on the container and then buy only as much as you need. Obey the manufacturer's instructions, keep the material out of the reach of children and pets and always be scrupulously careful to wash your hands (and any utensils) after use. Do not contaminate any source of water, particularly ponds, streams and ditches; fish can be affected even by diluted poisons.

Avoid spraying in windy conditions, which will spread the materials to places where you do not want them. Do not spray plants in flower, when there is a real risk of harming bees and many other nectar-feeding or pollinating insects; but if you must do so, always try to arrange such spraying in the evening.

Safe disposal is as important as safe storage. Solid remains should be sealed firmly in their containers and put in the trashcan; empty containers can go there too, but should be thoroughly rinsed out first. Surplus liquids must be effectively diluted before disposal and should then be emptied into an outside drain.

By following the guidelines given here it is possible to

use effective garden pest control methods without causing any harm to wildlife. For further information contact the organizations listed on page 156.

PREDATORS

THE MOST DIFFICULT CONCEPT for many bird gardeners to grasp is the relationship between garden birds and their predators—the other birds (or animals) which kill and eat them or rob their nests of eggs and young. To many people, wild creatures are "nice" or "nasty"; understandable though this may be, it is a fundamentally wrong way to look at nature. Predators and their prey exist in balance with one another, except where man introduces unnatural or artificial factors into the equation, and the numbers of predators are a reflection of the amount of prey available to them. Predators do not actually "control" the numbers of their prey species, as is often supposed. Nor is predation "cruel"—there is really no difference between a chickadee catching and eating a caterpillar, and a sharp-skinned hawk raiding a bird table.

If you live in an area where hawks occur, they will almost inevitably be attracted to a busy feeding station and a smash-and-grab raid on your bird table may well become a regular, even daily, event. This may distress you, but there is nothing you can do about it. You must accept it as perfectly normal and, indeed, realize that by

A cat's natural instinct is to hunt prey, and this kitten attempting to catch a dove (right) shows the problem common to bird and pet lovers. The main problem is not necessarily one of predation, but there may be sufficient disturbance to keep many bird species away from otherwise suitable areas.

providing food which concentrates many small birds in one area, you are in effect providing food for hawks. Their predation on small birds is only one of a series of natural factors, including starvation and disease, which results in high mortality, especially among inexperienced birds in their first winter.

Cat control

Fortunately, though, natural predators are relatively scarce in the garden and it is also likely that we will see very little of their comings and goings. Cats, however, are another matter. They are not natural predators since they occur in unnaturally high numbers, at a much greater density than would be possible for a wild predator. Nor

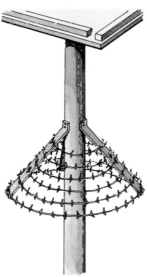

A barbed—wire skirt (above), or inverted cone, prevents predators such as rats, cats and squirrels reaching the food table.

If cats are fitted with a collar and bell, this will warn birds of their approach and prevents predation. The collar (above) should be elasticated to prevent strangulation should the cat get caught on an obstruction.

are they in any way limited by a natural food supply since they are domesticated and fed by us.

It is exceptionally difficult to keep cats out of gardens without resorting to the erection of close-mesh fencing or all sorts of anti-cat devices such as wires and broken glass along the tops of walls, which are not only unsightly but also tend to upset the neighbors! Commercial cat-repellents are often quite effective in the short term, but of course are expensive since they have to be used more or less continuously. All sorts of ingenious methods have been used to keep cats away from bird tables and feeders, including wire skirts below the table and projecting wires around about; feeders should certainly be situated as far away as possible from likely jumping-off points in trees, on walls and so on. Probably the best and simplest way to lessen the numbers of deaths caused by cats is to fit them with collars and bells.

Bird control

Magpies, jays and crows are all expert nest finders and for part of the year take the eggs and young of small birds. Crows are likely to do so only in large, quiet gardens since they are very wary birds, but jays may do so in well-timbered areas and magpies almost anywhere. Since magpies cause more argument and more concern than almost any other garden predator—cats included—let us consider the case for and against them.

Magpies are partial and seasonal predators: for most of the year they feed mainly on invertebrates and a variety of other foods, and only rarely kill birds. Most probably never do so at all. Their nest-robbing activities occur over a relatively short period and even then probably provide only a very small part of their diet. It is true that they may clean out a lot of nests in a small area, but their victims can withstand even heavy predation of this sort and will almost always move elsewhere and nest again. Any apparent decline or disappearance is, therefore, likely to be only temporary and in the long term the total numbers will not be affected. The situation is continuously monitored by the wildlife trusts and there is no evidence of a decline attributable to the activities of predators, and certainly none which correlates to increasing numbers of magpies.

As with hawks, so with magpies: you should learn to accept their nest raids as natural and inevitable, however much that may distress you at the moment when it happens. It is quite proper, of course, to take action against magpies and indeed jays and crows, using legal methods (see page 10). However, magpie control is hardly justifiable in the majority of situations, although exceptional circumstances can sometimes make it necessary.

FOOD AND FEEDERS

NOBODY KNOWS FOR CERTAIN when man consciously began to feed birds around his dwelling place, but it must have been going on for thousands of years—no doubt developing quite naturally through the habits of some species which scavenged around the homesteads. It may always have been done for purely altruistic reasons, but it has also been done to catch birds for keeping as pets—or for the pot. Nowadays, feeding birds is standard practice in many countries.

FEEDING BIRDS

PROVIDING FOOD ATTRACTS BIRDS and gives many people a lot of pleasure (which is no bad reason for doing it), but does it really have any conservation value? This is a difficult question to answer, not least because it is very difficult to measure what effect feeding has on the numbers of small birds. However, it is quite reasonable to assume that it is very beneficial to some species, at least in periods of prolonged severe weather and, especially, prolonged snow cover. Birds will very quickly find regular and reliable sources of food and will return to them again and again; they may come to rely on them, so it is very important, in hard weather at least, to continue a feeding program once you have started it.

It is not necessary to feed birds all through the year.

Some features of the ideal bird garden (below). The old tree stump with food crammed in cracks and a central hole makes an ideal low level, natural bird table (but is open to predation or unwanted visitors). The table, which is on a long pole, has a plastic sleeve to prevent cats from climbing up, and the inverted tin higher up will deter squirrels. The suspended nut basket is a further attraction.

nut basket

inverted tin

old tree stump

plastic sleeve

In winter, fallen fruit left on the ground or stored and then put out later is welcomed by birds such as these starlings (left). It is also a favorite food of blackbirds and other thrushes.

The birdbath (below) is a must for birds' bathing and drinking, as is the pond, which is provided with a suitable twiggy perch and stones for birds to stand on when drinking. The bucket of water and tap allow water to trickle or drip into the pond creating ripples or sounds which further attract birds to the pond. The perch on the ground is a favorite of robins and flycatchers, as it gives them a clear view. Note that the suspended feeder in the tree has fabric protecting the branch from damage by the string or wire.

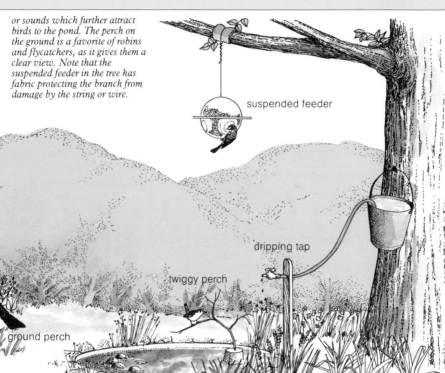

suspended feeder

bird bath

dripping tap

twiggy perch

ground perch

Natural food supplies should be readily available from spring to fall and, importantly, are the resources to which birds turn when feeding their young. Feeding in the garden is, therefore, unnecessary (and indeed not recommended) outside the winter months. Water on the other hand, can be made available all the year round, and is especially important during very cold weather.

Before discussing food and feeders in detail there are a few basic points to bear in mind. The first concerns 'competition' at feeders. Many people resent the bullying, over-confident attitudes of starlings or the abundance of house sparrows and feral pigeons. You cannot seriously hope to exclude any of these birds altogether, but you can manage them to some extent. Some feeders are accessible by holes only „or by spaces in mesh surrounds, which can exclude pigeons and starlings at least, and sometimes house sparrows. Unfortunately, though, a hole which is too small foiⁿa starling will also keep out evening grosbeaks. A rather better solution is probably to try to maintain two or three different feeding stations at once, well spaced out if possible, and to separate different kinds of food. This allows more individual birds to feed at the same time with some segregation—but it isn't foolproof!

Gray squirrels are fun to watch, but even a feeder well out of jumping range of a tree or wall may prove accessible to them. An inverted metal flange two-thirds of the way up the post of a bird table, with a plastic drainpipe placed like a sleeve over the post below it, is an effective and simple way of keeping gray squirrels at bay.

It is important to keep feeding stations reasonably clear of rotting food and to clean away old scraps so as to avoid the risk of disease and infection; do not allow uneaten food to lie around on the ground, where it is likely to attract rats and mice. The odd field mouse will probably be a welcome visitor, but lots of house mice and certainly lots of brown rats will not. Rats, incidentally, also carry a strong risk of introducing *salmonellosis*, which can cause heavy and distressing mortality among garden birds. Ideally, feeding sites should be moved once or twice during the winter and the feeders thoroughly cleaned in spring.

WHAT TO FEED — AND WHERE

THE SIMPLEST WAY TO FEED BIRDS is to scatter bread and other scraps on the ground, on a windowsill or on a flat roof. This almost invariably attracts hordes of house sparrows, starlings and pigeons, but it is also very useful in attracting some species which hardly ever visit bird tables or other feeders. Its big disadvantage is that it may also attract rats and mice. It is generally better to concentrate feeding at two or three sites, using a bird table and other feeding devices. This makes general hygiene easier, enables you to provide food close to the cover which is important to some species, means better protection from marauding cats and, last but not least, provides you with a much better chance of actually watching your guests. Ground-feeders can be provided with a small amount of food below bird tables and will, of course, be useful for the frequent spillages.

The basics

Many people believe that white bread is bad for birds—this is not so, but it can be hard and therefore very difficult for birds to break up and swallow, so it should be soaked in water first. The same general rule applies to other kinds of bread, all of which are very acceptable to many species. Cookies, cake remnants, cooked pastry leftovers and all the crumbs which accumulate in breadboxes, cookie tins etc are all worth putting out. Remember that most garden birds have very small mouths, so break it all up.

The list of kitchen scraps you can put out is almost endless. Small pieces of cheese are a favorite with many birds; so are bits of fat and, as a special treat, suet. Suet can be provided in small pieces, as a block which chickadees and nuthatches can chip away at (it is best to secure it by wire, or hang it from a convenient branch), or rammed into a hanging container. Many people push bits into cracks in trees for titmice and woodpeckers, or even create special feeding stations for them on old tree stumps. Suet, lard or dripping also forms the basis of the popular "bird cake": it is melted down and poured over a mixture of seeds, dried fruit, nuts, cake crumbs, cheese and virtually anything else you care to add. When hardened, this can be placed on a bird table, hung up in a container or crammed into a hole in a stump or tree-trunk. The proportions of the bird cake are roughly $1/2$ lb of fat to 1 lb of mixture.

Bones too attract titmice, nuthatches and woodpeckers, as well as starlings, either for the fat and meat left clinging to them or for the marrow inside. They are best hung up, and care should be taken with broken bones (especially poultry bones) left on the ground if you have a dog or a cat. Odd pieces of meat are relished by many birds. At least some should be minced up for small insectivorous birds like winter wrens. Minced meat has also been recorded as being eaten by birds like snipe and Virginia and Carolina rail in hard weather. Incidentally, commercially available cat and dog foods can also be put out for many small birds. Bacon rind, cut into small pieces, cooked or uncooked, is another firm favorite. Many people ask whether the salt content of bacon (and

indeed other foods) is harmful to birds, but there is no evidence to suggest that the amounts present have any ill effects. Many of these meaty foods will help small insectivorous birds, which generally have the hardest time finding enough to eat in severe weather, as long as what you provide is broken down into very small fragments. The so-called "ants' eggs" (really pupae and larvae) which you can buy very cheaply in pet stores are also very helpful to these species. If you can obtain them, mealworms (flour beetle larvae) are also very useful. All species of birds studied for food preferences have been partial to mealworms.

The titbits

Nuts of course, are very popular. Almost any kind will do, but peanuts are the best (not, however, the excessively salted variety available in bars etc), either strung up in their shells, placed in a nut basket, suspended in the mesh bags in which they now come prepacked, or simply scattered on the bird table. Peanuts can be bought in bulk from many pet stores and commercial bird food suppliers; they sell like the proverbial hot cakes, so lay in a good supply.

Titmice, nuthatches and even downy woodpeckers will delight you with their antics where nuts are hung up for them. They will even come right up against windows. Siskins (where they occur in winter) will also be attracted by nuts. Unfortunately, house sparrows are also very fond of nuts and will very quickly learn how to get at them. One way to prevent them from taking more than their fair share is to hang the nut basket inside a glass jar, leaving only the base of the basket accessible. Titmice and siskins can cope with this, but sparrows find it rather difficult. Half a coconut can be suspended for chickadees and nuthatches, and once emptied, the shell makes a useful bird cake container. Dessicated coconut should *not* be put out as it may swell up inside the bird.

Many kinds of mixed, small vegetables and dried peas, lentils etc are useful additions to the menu; dried fruits, especially currants and sultanas, are also firm favorites with many species. Whole or half apples are much appreciated by robins and orioles and many other species. Leave a few windfalls and any damaged apples for the birds, and if you can, set aside a small proportion of your crop against the possibility of hard weather later on. Oats, oatmeal, corn flakes, puppy meal and all kinds of "bird seed" can also be put out—a seed hopper is recommended to avoid too much spillage. Most commercial wild bird foods contain a high proportion of seeds among their many ingredients, and can be recommended; they sometimes lead to strange things growing in the garden in spring too! Sunflower seeds are perhaps the most popular

FEEDING REQUIREMENTS

Green-backed heron: Fish, frogs and invertebrates

Mallard: Vegetative matter, nymphs and larvae of aquatic flies and beetles

Wood duck: Acorns, beech nuts, water plants

Killdeer: Beetles, grasshoppers, caterpillars, ants, crustaceans and invertebrates

Red-tailed hawk: Rodents, snakes, lizards and rabbits

American kestrel: Mainly insects, small mammals, reptiles

Northern bobwhite: Exclusively seeds

California quail: Plant leaves and seeds of legumes

Ring-necked pheasant: Corn, grass, seeds and small insects

Mourning dove: Grass seeds, grain crops and variety of other seeds

Common ground dove: Mainly seeds of grasses and forbs; some insects

Barn owl: Rodents

Great-horned owl: Skunks, rats, squirrels, grouse, weasels, snakes and insects

Eastern screech owl: Worms, crayfish, voles, mice, small birds, insects

Chimney swift: Flying insects taken on the wing

Ruby-throated hummingbird: Flower nectar, tree sap, some insects

Anna's hummingbird: Flower nectar, tree sap, some insects

Black-chinned hummingbird: Flower nectar and small insects

Red-bellied woodpecker: Acorns and other tree fruit; some insects

Red-headed woodpecker: Acorns, wild berries, fruit and nuts; insects and small invertebrates

Common flicker: Ants; other insects and berries

Hairy woodpecker: Mainly insects and spiders; some fruits and seeds

Downy woodpecker: Insects, berries and seeds

Eastern kingbird: Winged insects like bees; occasionally berries

Eastern phoebe: Mainly insects and spiders; occasionally berries

Least flycatcher: Exclusively insects and spiders

Tree swallow: Mainly winged insects

Violet-green swallow: Exclusively insects

Purple martin: Insects caught on the wing

Cliff swallow: Insects; some berries

Barn swallow: Mainly insects; some berries

Blue jay: Acorns, beech nuts, tree mast, insects, birds' eggs, nestlings, voles and mice

Black-billed magpie: Insects, seeds, berries, eggs, mice and carrion

Common crow: Animal and vegetable matter

Tufted titmouse: Mainly insects; also seeds and berries

Black-capped chickadee: Mainly insects and invertebrates; also seeds and berries

Carolina chickadee: Mainly insects; also seeds, berries and other fruit

Bushtit: Mainly insects; also seeds and berries

Western bluebird: Mainly insects, spiders and other invertebrates; also berries

Wood thrush: Insects, worms, invertebrates, larvae, berries and seeds

Brown creeper: Insects; also spiders and seeds

White-breasted nuthatch: Insects, spiders, nuts, seeds and berries

Red-breasted nuthatch: Insects, egg cases, pine seeds, berries and fruit

Winter wren: Invertebrates, insects and spiders

House wren: Insects, spiders and larval forms

Carolina wren: Insects and all types of invertebrates; also seeds

Blue-gray gnatcatcher: Mainly insects; other invertebrates including spiders

Ruby-crowned kinglet: Insects, spiders, egg cases; some fruit

Golden-crowned kinglet: Insects, spiders and some berries

Eastern bluebird: Insects ; also berries, fruit and seeds

American robin: Earthworms, grubs, larvae, insects, spiders; also berries, fruit and seeds

Loggerhead shrike: Large insects, small mammals, small birds and their young

Gray catbird: 50% animal matter, 50% berries, fruit and seeds

Mockingbird: Wild berries, seeds, insects and invertebrates

Brown thrasher: Insects, small invertebrates, some fruit and seeds

Cedar waxwing: Mainly berries and seeds; also insects

Veery: Insects, spiders and other invertebrates; also snails and berries

Hermit thrush: Insects, spiders, small snails, berries and seeds

White-eyed vireo: Insects, spiders and other invertebrates; also berries

Red-eyed vireo: Mainly insects, spiders and other invertebrates

Orange-crowned warbler: Mainly insects and spiders; also seeds and berries

Black and white warbler: Insects, eggs, larvae, pupae, also spiders

Yellow-rumped warbler: Spiders, insects, berries, fruit and seeds

Yellow-throated warbler: Mainly insects and spiders

Yellow warbler: Mainly insects; also berries

Common yellowthroat: Insects

American redstart: Insects, spiders, fruit and seeds

Rose-breasted grosbeak: Insects and fruit; also fruit, seeds and cherry blossom

Northern cardinal: Mainly seeds and fruit; also insects and spiders

Blue grosbeak: Seeds, berries and fruit; also insects, spiders, egg cases and larvae

Indigo bunting: Mainly insects and spiders; also seeds and fruit

Painted bunting: Insects, spiders, berries and seeds

Rufous-sided towhee: Seeds, fruit and insects

Brown towhee: Seeds, fruit, variety of insects

Savannah sparrow: Mainly seeds; also insects

Song sparrow: Mainly seeds; also insects and invertebrates

Tree sparrow: Mainly insects and some seeds

Field sparrow: Seeds and insects; also berries

Chipping sparrow: Seeds, insects, spiders and other invertebrates

Dark-eyed junco: Mainly insects and seeds

White-throated sparrow: Weed seeds and insects

White-crowned sparrow: Insects and berries; also seeds

House finch: Seeds, fruit and some insects

Purple finch: Mainly seeds and fruit; also insects

Northern oriole: Mainly insects and spiders; also fruit and seeds

American goldfinch: Mainly seeds; also insects

Scott's oriole: Insects, various fruits and flower nectar

Orchard oriole: Mainly insects, spiders and other invertebrates; also seeds and berries

Brown-headed cowbird: Grain, seeds, berries and other fruit; some insects

Boat-tailed grackle: Seeds, fruit, insects, small mammals, fish

Brewer's blackbird: Grain, seeds and fruit; also insects and invertebrates

Common grackle: Insects, grass seeds, worms, eggs and young birds

Eastern meadowlark: Insects, grubs, grass seeds and weed seeds

Red-winged blackbird: Insects, and seeds

Fox sparrow: Insects, seeds and fruit

Dickcissel: Grass seeds, grain and insects

Red crossbill: Pine seeds, other fruit and seeds

Evening grosbeak: All types of seeds and fruit

Pine siskin: Seeds and some insects

Common redpoll: Mainly insects and fruit

seeds of all, much loved by evening grosbeaks in particular—they are usually included in wild bird mixtures, but can be bought separately. You can, of course, grow your own and enjoy the sunflowers themselves before they become bird food.

One of the great pleasures of feeding birds is that there is almost no limit to the menu: follow the guidelines given here, but experiment with your own ideas too.

ALL KINDS OF FEEDERS

THE CLASSIC BIRD TABLE is a simple, flat board mounted on a post. It is actually available in a wide variety of forms, from very simple to rustic (and sometimes quite awful)—but the birds have no eye for what may please *you* and their requirements are very simple. Whether you buy a ready-made table or make one yourself, following the basic instructions given here, is really up to you. Incidentally, there is no reason why a plastic table should not do just as well as a more traditional wooden one.

Ideally, a bird table should sit securely on a firm post approximately 5 ft above the ground, not too far from cover, but out of the jumping range (from walls and trees) of cats and gray squirrels. It should have a roof to keep the food fairly dry (the roof can also incorporate a food hopper) and should have a low surrounding rim to avoid too much spillage of food on to the ground below. Gaps in the rim or holes bored in the table itself will assist in draining off rainwater. It is also possible to place bird tables on walls or window-ledges by using metal or wooden brackets, or to hang them up by cords or chains.

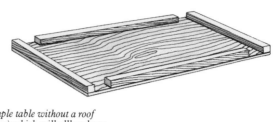

A simple table without a roof (above) which will alllow large birds access to the food on the plate.

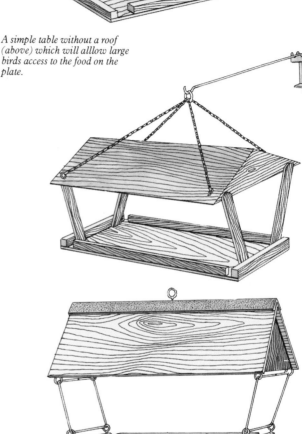

Two types of hanging tables (above). The latter with a removable tray which is suspended from the roof.

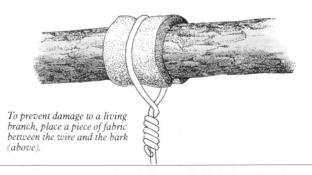

An exploded diagram of a typical bird table (below). Remember that the roof segments should overlap to cut down leaks onto the base plate, and that the coaming is incomplete to allow easy drainage and cleaning.

To prevent damage to a living branch, place a piece of fabric between the wire and the bark (above).

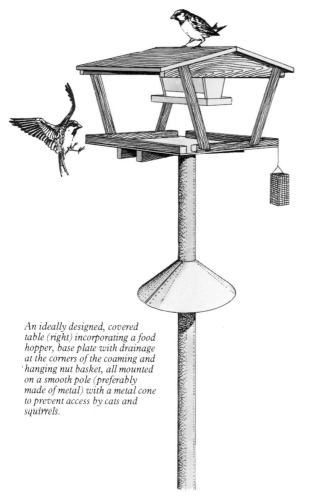

An ideally designed, covered table (right) incorporating a food hopper, base plate with drainage at the corners of the coaming and hanging nut basket, all mounted on a smooth pole (preferably made of metal) with a metal cone to prevent access by cats and squirrels.

A badly constructed table (right), commonly found for sale in many garden centers. The nesting hole will cause disputes among certain species; there are no gaps in the coaming for drainage or cleaning, and the rough surface of the pole will allow predators to attack feeding birds, or squirrels to raid the table.

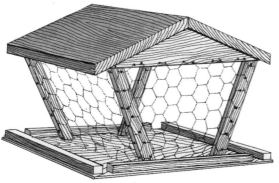

A table especially designed for the smaller species (above). The wire mesh keeps the larger birds away from the food, but allows smaller species to move freely through the holes.

Many species like to perch on a good vantage point before venturing onto tables, or down to water. A strategically placed perch (above) will help them to make up their minds.

Nuts can be strung from the sides and nut baskets and other feeding devices can be suspended from them.

Purpose-built metal or plastic nut and scrap baskets come in a variety of shapes and sizes and are available quite cheaply from many sources. Many stores now sell nuts prepacked in inexpensive sausage-shaped bags and these have proved highly popular and very successful. They have the advantage that they can be hung almost anywhere. There is now an enormous range of garden bird equipment available, including food hoppers, chickadee bells, windowsill trays and so on, some of them incorporating several features at once and others with covered feeding areas accessible only to chickadees.

You can, of course, make your own feeding devices. A chickadee bell—which is basically some sort of inverted container for fat-based bird cake and the like—can be made from half a coconut shell, an empty yogurt container or even an old jam-jar. Other jars of various sizes can be mounted or suspended horizontally and will provide excellent feeders. You can also create sheltered ground feeding stations by using simple screens which will not only protect the food you put down, but also give some protection from predators.

One further tip: some garden birds, like Carolina wrens, do not come very readily to feeders and although they may come to food on the ground they really prefer to feed under cover and in thick vegetation. Heavy snow cover greatly reduces their options, so be prepared to clear snow away for them and open up areas of undergrowth and hedge bottoms for them. Small supplies of fat, cheese and "ants' eggs" can also be useful.

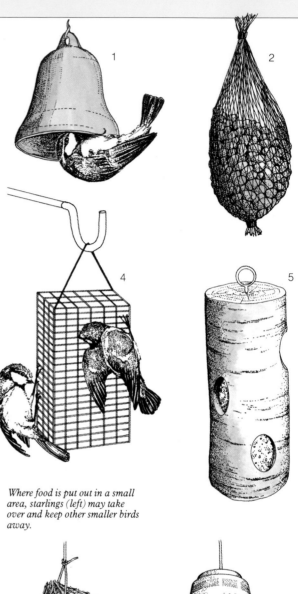

Where food is put out in a small area, starlings (left) may take over and keep other smaller birds away.

Once the chickadees have eaten the coconut, the empty shell can be filled with "bird cake" (above).

Similarly, this empty plastic yogurt carton (above) can be filled with fat, nuts and seed, and then suspended.

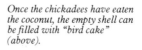

The chickadee bell (1) is very popular when filled with "bird cake." The nut bag (2) is suitable for finches and chickadees. The seed hopper (3) means you can put out a lot of nuts and seed at once, rather than constantly renewing supplies. Nut baskets (4) are very popular, but make sure there are no sharp edges or points, as these can damage birds' legs. A simple device for "bird cake" is the birch log (5) drilled with holes and then filled with fat, a favorite of woodpeckers and nuthatches. Another type of hopper (6) is the globe — this also keeps the food dry and can only be used by small birds. A nut feeder (7) and drinking cup on a long plastic pole.

A hole bored in the middle of a tree stump (above) and filled with suet, fat and seeds makes an ideal feeding station.

A suspended glass jar (above) filled with seeds and nuts will entice chickadees and finches, and also keeps the food dry.

An alternative method is to secure the jar in the fork of a tree (above). Clear glass allows the birds to see the food.

Peanuts still in their kernels and threaded on to a piece of string (above) makes the chickadees work harder and is fun to watch.

HOMES FOR ALL

HOWEVER YOU MANAGE THE TREES in your garden, natural hole nest-sites are always at a premium. In many gardens there will be none at all. Nestboxes provide an ideal substitute and while their basic design caters for hole-nesters, boxes can also be adapted to suit other species, particularly those which like ledges and sheltered cavities. Here are some of the main factors to bear in mind when considering nestboxes.

BASIC CONSIDERATIONS

NESTBOXES CAN BE FITTED to walls or trees, according to what is available. There is no hard and fast rule about how high they should be placed, but "out of reach" (of humans and cats) is a good rule of thumb. Around 10 ft up is fine, but probably no lower than 6½ ft. The sheltered side of a wall or tree is best, but many boxes are also in exposed situations. It is always best to place the box so that it faces away from the prevailing wind or rain direction and also away from the greatest heat of the sun,

in other words not facing due south. A sheltered and reasonably well hidden situation is necessary for open-fronted boxes which are used by robins, phoebes and barn swallows.

Once a box is in use, it should be disturbed as little as possible: it is best not to examine the contents at all, but if for any reason you must do so, exercise great care and make your visits as brief and infrequent as possible. You may also realize at some point that something has gone wrong, and a quick inspection may reveal deserted eggs or even dead young birds. You may have caused desertion yourself by disturbing the box too much, but there is also a chance that cold weather may have caused the adults to desert eggs, or a failure in the food supply has led to the starvation of the young.

Direct predation from cats, weasels, squirrels or even blue jays is also possible. Strategically placed wires or obstacles may deter cats, but squirrels are notoriously hard to keep away from nestboxes. Metal cones at the entrance holes of boxes have stopped weasel predation

To reduce the size of a nestbox entrance, and thereby make the box more suitable for a smaller species, a length of wood (which doubles as a perch) can be nailed across it (left).

If the hole in a nestbox is slightly too large, house sparrows (right) will take it over. While not always unwelcome guests, they can deprive birds such as blue tits for which these nestboxes are intended.

When suitably placed in the fork of a tree, or low down in vegetation, and where water cannot get in, old kettles or jugs (above) make ideal nesting sites for robins.

When attaching a nestbox to a tree, be sure to place it away from side branches so that predators, such as cats (right) cannot get near them.

(the animals cannot climb around them to get at the holes) and metal plates fitted around the entrance frustrate most squirrels, who have to enlarge the hole by gnawing before they can get inside. Woodpeckers may be deterred by this method too, but can, of course, break into a wooden box from any direction. It is best to accept that a certain amount of predation is inevitable. Wasps, bees and earwigs may colonize a nestbox. Earwigs cause the birds no problem and can be left alone; wasps and bees are probably best left alone too (although a professional bee keeper can remove a swarm for you) and rather than meddle with them, it would be better to put up another box nearby.

Once a box has been used, there remains the question of whether or not to clear it out. The nest débris, plus perhaps old food remains or even a rotting dead chick, will attract insects and bird parasites, some of which may be harmful to next year's young, so it is best to clean out used boxes, but not until early spring. Things should be left as they are during the winter as nestboxes may be used by chickadees and sometimes bluebirds for roosting—or even may be occupied by flying squirrels and white-footed mice, who make enjoyable winter occupants. Remove the box completely, clear out all the contents and pour boiling water over the interior to kill off any remaining parasites. Check for repairs to the lid or sides and make these good. A wood preservative (but *not* creosote) can be applied and will lengthen the life of a wooden box. Given proper care and attention it should last for many years and give excellent service.

As with bird tables and feeding devices, so with

nestboxes: there are many different kinds on the market in the basic design range, some perfectly acceptable, but others hopelessly inadequate. Bear in mind the size and hole position mentioned previously and look carefully at fixing methods. Wooden boxes are generally better than plastic ones, although some of the latter have proved very successful. Remember that birds are not influenced by style—only by certain simple requirements, which are usually not to difficult to provide.

NESTBOXES IN DETAIL

THE BASIC NESTBOX is about 10in high and 6in deep, with a sloping, hinged roof (or a removable front panel) and an entrance hole, near the top, on either the front or the side. It exists in various styles, or can be made very easily from a plank of wood about 4³/₄ft long, 6in wide and ¹/₂in thick. The internal floor size should be at least 4in x 4in and the entrance hole should be positioned about 5in from the floor.

The box is best secured by battens, or via an elongated rear panel, preferably using screws. Nails will do, but should be the galvanized rather than the wire kind. Among the birds likely to use such a box are house wrens, chickadees, tree swallows, house finches, titmice, and the like. By confining the entrance hole to a diameter of 1in for house wrens, 1¹/₄in for chickadees and titmice and 1(33¹/₃in for tree swallows and house finches, larger, so-called "harmful" species can be kept out.

To attract larger species more specific box dimensions

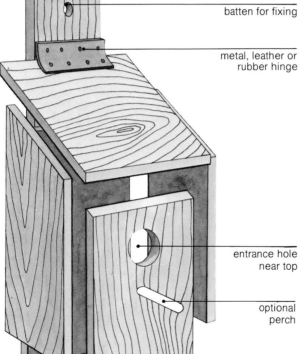

batten for fixing

metal, leather or
rubber hinge

entrance hole
near top

optional
perch

drainage holes in
underneath

An exploded view of a typical nestbox (above) showing the ease of construction. The hinged lid allows viewing of the contents.

The perch will give good views of the adults before entry.

The metal plate (above) stops birds like the sparrows enlarging the hole.

This open-fronted box (above) is ideal for species like the least flycatcher and robin.

Always try to position the box facing away from the prevailing wind and, if possible, tilted slightly

downward (above) to prevent rain from entering and soaking or even drowning the nestlings.

are necessary. For information as to the precise box and entrance hole dimensions required by individual species please refer to the appropriate entry in the following "Directory of 100 Garden Birds."

Some species, such as the robin, phoebe and barn swallow, just need a shelf on which to place their nest. A flat 6in x 6in square board will suffice. A canopy over the top will help to keep out the worst of the weather, and a slight ridge around the edge of the board will help to hold the nesting material in place.

Boxes have been developed for a wide range of other birds, not all of which occur in gardens. There is now a standard design for screech owls which has proved very successful. It should be at least 10ft above ground level, preferably more, and should be placed at an angle of

about 45 degrees to the horizontal, either on a main trunk, in a substantial fork or on the underside of a large limb. The box itself should have a 10in x 10in base with 24in high sides and a 4in diameter entrance hole about 20in above the floor. Screech owls are likely to nest in any well timbered garden, and often in gardens well inside city limits.

Barn owls are not garden birds in the normal sense, but may well occur around large properties, farm building complexes, factory sites and the like. They have declined in many areas and one reason for this is the loss of nest-sites through the removal of old trees or the demolition or modernization of old buildings.

A box could be erected for them in a dark corner of a suitable quiet outbuilding, or in the upper part of a

To avoid damage to trees use a leather strap (above) to fix nestboxes to them.

If a suitable angled branch is not available, an owl box can be fixed at an angle (above).

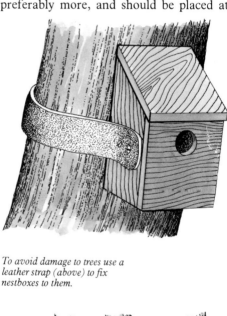

A fork of a tree is an ideal site for an open-fronted box (above).

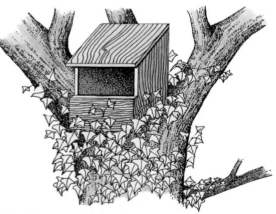

A screech owl box strapped to the underside of a branch (above). It may also be used by doves.

modern barn—wherever the site, it is important that they are free from disturbance. Feeding primarily on small rodents, especially rats and mice, they are worth having around. Kestrel boxes are really only suitable for people with large, rather open areas adjacent to their houses or places of work. Kestrel boxes can be placed on trees or even on poles in open fields.

Barn swallows, cliff swallows and purple martins are all often associated with human habitations and can all be attracted by the provision of the right kinds of nesting places. Perhaps the best known of all nestboxes is the purple martin house. This large structure with up to 30 compartments or more can be purchased from a variety of outlets. An equally successful approach is to place special hollowed out gourds, with entrance holes drilled in the appropriate places, on a crossbeam.

On the other hand, swallows simply require a suitable ledge or shelf in a porch outbuilding, garage or garden shed, which can be designed and fitted for them quite easily; but remember to leave a window or door open for them to come and go, or to make an entrance hole for them in a building which has to remain closed or which is likely to be locked up for any length of time.

Cliff swallows build a gourd-shaped nest of mud which is affixed to walls, almost always just below a gutter or the eaves, but sometimes in the angle at the end of a gable. They are highly colonial and often nest in large numbers at traditional sites, but new colonists can be attracted by using the custom-built artificial nests advertised in several ornithological magazines. One of the main problems with cliff swallows is the mess they make on walls and windows, prompting many people to set about removing their nests. A better solution is to place a 6 in board below the nest to catch most of the droppings.

A barn owl box (above) suitably placed near a hole in an old outbuilding will attract these birds. This bird (below) is leaving the nest behind the bricks.

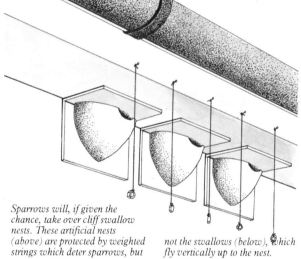

Sparrows will, if given the chance, take over cliff swallow nests. These artificial nests (above) are protected by weighted strings which deter sparrows, but not the swallows (below), which fly vertically up to the nest.

Another thing which worries people is the way in which house sparrows try to take over cliff swallow nests; it is difficult to do much to help, but some success has been achieved by hanging lengths of wool vertically downwards to upset the sparrows without affecting the swallows, as the latter, unlike the sparrows, swoop up to the nest from underneath.

Brown creepers nest in crevices in big trees or behind pieces of loose bark and are always possible breeders in large, well-timbered gardens.

Space does not permit mention of all the other species which might possibly be attracted, but further details are available in the publications listed on pages 156 and 157. Birds are not the only creatures to use boxes, and at a time when bats are finding it difficult to find undisturbed roosting places there are good reasons for putting up one or two bat boxes in the garden.

A kestrel box (above) should be placed 20–30 ft up on a pole, or tree. The roof should be waterproofed.

Bats also need roosting sites. Place the box (above) 12–15ft up in a tree.

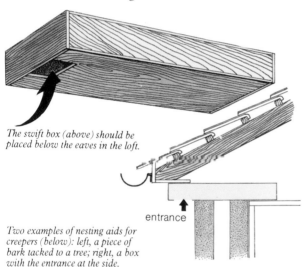

The swift box (above) should be placed below the eaves in the loft.

entrance

Two examples of nesting aids for creepers (below): left, a piece of bark tacked to a tree; right, a box with the entrance at the side.

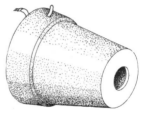

Wrens will nest in a variety of objects such as flowerpots, coconuts and pipes (above, right). They also use conventional nests (below).

DIRECTORY
of 100 garden birds

How To Use The Directory

ATTRACTING BIRDS to your garden requires not only a fair degree of gardening skill but also a working knowledge of the particular demands and characteristics of individual birds. The following directory contains detailed information on distribution, plumage, size, preferred habitats, nesting habits, food requirements and sources and much more for 100 species.

The directory provides both comprehensive ornithological information *and* readily accessible details for easy and quick reference. Four birds — house wren, northern mockingbird, northern cardinal and northern oriole — have been selected for special features. The remaining 96 species appear on a single page format.

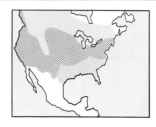

Outline maps of North America give detailed distribution information.
Taking into account migratory patterns, the maps show summer distribution (in green), winter distribution (in diagonal hatching) and all year distribution (in green with diagonal hatching).

Summer distribution

Winter distribution

All year distribution

FALCONS : FALCONIDAE

AMERICAN KESTREL *Falco sparverius*

This is th[e] commone[st] found in [...] although [...] more ope[n] hovers [...] suburba[...] when p[...] the shar[...] kleee ca[...] enticed [...] by the [...]

THE MOST COMMON FALCON i[...] species is found from coast to co[...] are yearlong residents but major [...] birds can be expected in the fall. [...] the south during the winter is re[...]

The smallest of our falcons, th[e...] only one exhibiting a russet br[...] marked by two distinct black [...] background. A terminal band of [...] males and females. The males ha[...] call is a piercing *kleeee, kleeee*[...] hunting is diagnostic.

A wide variety of habitats a[...] long as there is open country it [...] at home hunting from atop a po[...] city highway, to a ledge in a hig[...] midwest and south, birds hov[...] are a typical sight.

Kestrels feed on a wide vari[...] mammals, occasionally small [...] During migration, dragonflie[...] of their diet.

Extensive nesting box prog[...] species (which is a hole neste[...] made structures. The box use[...] to the wood duck box, being l[...] high. An elliptical opening 4 [...] keep out most intruding raco[...] a tree at the edge of an open a[...] from 20 to 40 ft up, although[...] occupied boxes lower do[...] protected with stain or pai[...] used—khaki and earthy ta[...] wood shavings on the floor [...]

FACTS AND FEATURES

11 in

Plumage Male: striped facial pattern; brown back; blue gray wing; reddish tail with terminal band. Female: foxy brown, less distinct head pattern.
Habitat Any open area, parks, farmland, prairie, desert.

Food Mainly insects (including dragonflies) small mammals, reptiles, occasionally small birds.
Nest Hole-nesting species. Takes over nest holes of woodpeckers or in natural tree or cliff cavity.

56

(2) Flight silhouettes are given for each species to enable easy identification in the air. Beneath the silhouette is the bill-to-tail measurement.

(3) The nest symbol (when ticked) indicates that the species will nest in a garden if the right environment is provided.

(4) The nestbox symbol (when ticked) indicates that the species will use a nestbox provided it is of the right type and size.

(5) The bird table symbol (when ticked) indicates that the species will come to a feeding area if the appropriate food is put out.

(6) The plant symbol (when ticked) indicates that certain plants will be a positive attractant for some species. Details of these plants can be found in the main entry for each relevant species.

(7) Family name, English and scientific.

(8) Species name, English and scientific.

(9) Main entry, containing comprehensive details of distribution, plumage, behaviour, breeding, nesting habits, calls and songs, migratory patterns and much more.

(10) 'Facts and features' box for easy reference. Containing distribution map, flight silhouette with bill to tail measurement, symbol panel and abbreviated information on plumage, habitat, food and nest.

(11) Specially commissioned artwork showing detailed plumage breakdown and, where necessary, showing the difference between male and female plumages.

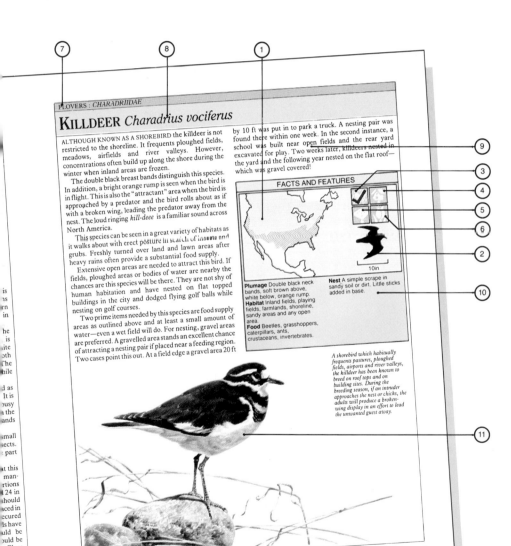

PLOVERS : *CHARADRIIDAE*

KILLDEER *Charadrius vociferus*

ALTHOUGH KNOWN AS A SHOREBIRD the killdeer is not restricted to the shoreline. It frequents ploughed fields, meadows, airfields and river valleys. However, concentrations often build up along the shore during the winter when inland areas are frozen.

The double black breast bands distinguish this species. In addition, a bright orange rump is seen when the bird is in flight. This is also the "attractant" area when the bird is approached by a predator and the bird rolls about as if with a broken wing, leading the predator away from the nest. The loud ringing *kill-deee* is a familiar sound across North America.

This species can be seen in a great variety of habitats as it walks about with erect posture in search of insects and grubs. Freshly turned over land and lawn areas after heavy rains often provide a substantial food supply.

Extensive open areas are needed to attract this bird. If fields, ploughed areas or bodies of water are nearby the chances are this species will be there. They are not shy of human habitation and have nested on flat topped buildings in the city and dodged flying golf balls while nesting on golf courses.

Two prime items needed by this species are food supply areas as outlined above and at least a small amount of water—even a wet field will do. For nesting, gravel areas are preferred. A gravelled area stands an excellent chance of attracting a nesting pair if placed near a feeding region. Two cases point this out. At a field edge a gravel area 20 ft by 10 ft was put in to park a truck. A nesting pair was found there within one week. In the second instance, a school was built near open fields and the rear yard excavated for play. Two weeks later, killdeers nested in the yard and the following year nested on the flat roof—which was gravel covered!

FACTS AND FEATURES

10in

Plumage Double black neck bands, soft brown above, white below, orange rump.
Habitat Inland fields, playing fields, farmlands, shoreline, sandy areas and any open area.
Food Beetles, grasshoppers, caterpillars, ants, crustaceans, invertebrates.

Nest A simple scrape in sandy soil or dirt. Little sticks added in base.

A shorebird which habitually frequents pastures, ploughed fields, airports and river valleys, the killdeer has been known to breed on roof tops and on building sites. During the breeding season, if an intruder approaches the nest or chicks, the adults will produce a broken-wing display in an effort to lead the unwanted guest away.

57

GREEN-BACKED HERON *Butorides striatus*

THIS SMALL HERON is an abundant summer resident throughout most of the United States and a permanent resident in areas such as the Gulf Coast and Florida.

Easily told by its size, this species has a rich chestnut neck contrasting with its white streaked throat and dark cap. Its name comes from the greenish sheen on the basically grayish back, that is exhibited in breeding plumage. Legs are a bright yellow-orange. The call is an unforgettable, loud *skeeow,* and while moving about, it flicks its tail. Young birds are heavily spotted and streaked.

As long as water is present, there is a chance this species will occur, from lake shore to wet grass swale. In southern areas, salt water sites such as mangrove swamps are also frequented. It can be overlooked as it sits and waits motionless for prey or slowly stalks through the grasses blending perfectly with the background. The nest is a loose jumble of sticks placed well up in a tree, preferably a maple tree. It is such a loose affair that the eggs can often be seen through the sticks from below.

Due to its abundance and adaptability to man's presence, this species will move into populated areas. Indeed, in several instances small ponds in the back yards of city homes, have been inhabited by this species during the summer.

A wet area is a must, with a small pond being ideal, and one other necessity appears to be some form of cover from which to hunt. Cattails can be encouraged to grow or shrubs and grasses planted for this purpose. Floating vegetation can also provide cover for young fish and frogs as well as the invertebrates that form the bulk of the birds' diet. If a grove of trees is fairly close by, it would increase the chances for nesting.

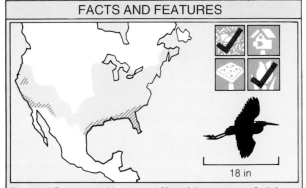

FACTS AND FEATURES

18 in

Plumage Dark cap; white streaked throat; chestnut neck; greenish gray back; bright yellow-orange legs.
Habitat Pond edges, swamps, wet swales; also at edge of salt water areas and in mangroves in the south.
Food Fish, frogs, invertebrates.

Nest A loose mass of sticks in deciduous trees in northern areas. The preference is for maple. In the south, mangroves are used.

Common and widespread, the green-backed heron is easily overlooked because of its skulking behavior. Recently, it has begun to move into urban areas especially where there is standing water and abundant vegetation.

MALLARD *Anas platyrhynchos*

♀

♂

Possibly the most abundant duck to be encountered within parks and gardens. It will nest some distance from water provided that there is an area for concealment of the nest.

PERHAPS THE BEST KNOWN DUCK in North America, this species is common throughout its range, which includes all of the contiguous 48 states and all but northernmost Canada. It also summers throughout Alaska.

The male is easily identified by the intense green head, yellow bill, white neck ring and chestnut chest. The female, although brown and tan overall, has a distinct tan head, yellowish bill with dark markings and a metallic blue patch in the wing (the speculum) bordered by white. This species interbreeds with a wide variety of ducks, but in particular the black duck, therefore, oddly marked ducks are sure to be encountered. In most instances the green of the head is exhibited at least as a crown stripe.

This species can be expected to occur anywhere there is open water, from town park to woodland lake. The nest is a deep dish shape, hidden in vegetation, quite often some distance from the water. The nest lining is of feathers and the female will often dive from the nest feigning injury if approached too closely. Ten to 12 eggs is the usual clutch. In the spring, lines of ducklings tagging after the female and stopping traffic as they cross city streets is not an uncommon occurrence.

Small pools can be excavated to attract this species, and anyone living near a lake edge, river or stream is sure to see them at some time. They tame down very easily and can be "trained" to show up at specific times for feeding. A trail of cracked corn from the water's edge to a desired feeding location can quickly be established. When a group takes up residence, in the form of deep grasses or shrubbery, nesting is bound to occur. Care should be taken never to feed damp grain to this species. Dampness can promote fungal growth, and some fungal forms can kill entire flocks when ingested.

FACTS AND FEATURES

23 in

Plumage Male: bright green head, yellow bill, white neck ring, gray body. Female: all mottled brown; orange bill with black smudges; blue wing patch.
Habitat Lakes, ponds, stream edges and wooded swamps. City parks and suburban areas.

Food Wide variety of vegetative matter; nymphs and larvae of aquatic flies and beetles.
Nest On the ground in protected site: grass clump, shrub base etc. Feather lined.

WOOD DUCK *Aix sponsa*

THIS IS A COMMON SPECIES of the eastern United States and fairly common along the extreme west coast from southern California to northern—Washington. Summer birds extend their range over into Canada in the east, midwest and far west. During the winter the majority of the population moves south.

The male is considered one of the most beautiful ducks in the world. In breeding plumage it is distinctive with an irridescent green head swept back into a long white streaked crest. This is offset by a vermillion eye and deep red and white bill. The female is a warm brown with a brown crest, and distinctive white eye ring that rounds off into a tear-drop mark behind the eye. In flight the squared-off long tail and head held drooping downward are distinctive.

A bird of woodland ponds and river backwaters, it can be very shy and one usually encounters it by hearing the high pitched *ooo--eek* of the female as it takes flight. Nesting is in a natural cavity high in a tree or in a nesting box placed out for them. The nest site is not always near the water, with some birds nesting up to a mile away. Nest sites can be as high as 40 ft up, quite a jump for the young when they hatch. Upon landing, they are led to the water by the female. Dump nesting, one female depositing its eggs in the nest of another, is a common occurrence.

This bird has shown how well it can adapt to nest boxes placed in a suitable habitat. In the 1950s the nesting populations were at a very low point. The nesting box program was undertaken and the population is presently at an all time high. If any sizable body of water is available a nesting box (10 in x 10 in x 24 in high with an eliptical hole 4 in wide by 3 in high and centered 20 in above the floor) placed on a post 2–5 ft above water level would attract possible breeding pairs. Sawdust should be placed in the bottom as a nest basis. The boxes can also be placed on trees (15–40 ft up) away from water as long as there is a wetland situation within quarter of a mile. All such areas will be explored by a pair before nesting occurs.

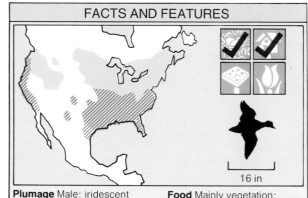

FACTS AND FEATURES

Plumage Male: iridescent green head with white face pattern; red and white bill; long tail. Female: light brown, darker on back, white tear drop eye marking.
Habitat Pond edges, wooded swamps, streams or in woodland interior.

Food Mainly vegetation: acorns, beech nuts, water plants; bulrushes, pondweed, water lily seeds.
Nest In a tree hole up to 40 ft off the ground. Usually within reach of water. Accepts nest boxes.

16 in

♂

If your garden has a small lake with well wooded margins. and is situated in the eastern states, you may encounter this attractive duck. The provision of nest boxes placed in trees will encourage breeding. The birds themselves are very agile and move easily among the trees.

RED-TAILED HAWK *Buteo jamaicensis*

THE COMMONEST LARGE HAWK in North America, most birds are year round residents except in the northernmost areas.

This is one of the most variable of the hawks as far as plumage is concerned. Adults of most forms can be told by the rusty red tail, but the dark "Harlan's" form of western Canada and Alaska lacks this and has a mottled gray-brown tail. In general the species is a large hawk, with dark "hood" appearance and many have a dark lower belly band. This feature can be lost in the southwest forms. This species is often seen soaring lazily over the plains or woodlands or perched on a telephone pole.

One reason for the abundance of this bird is its ability to adapt to various habitats. In the east, any significant section of woodlands can have a nesting pair, even within major cities. In the west, barren canyonlands have nesting birds on cliff faces, and in the desert, large cacti often support the nest. Food consists of a wide range of rodents from mice up to rabbit size. Occasionally snakes are taken, including venomous forms.

Depending on the area where one lives, the key requirements to attract this species are available hunting areas in the form of extensive fields or open areas and woodland or other suitable nesting area. Birds often come to regular feeding sites where carcasses from animals killed along the road have been placed.

For pairs to breed, woodlands or other suitable nesting habitat and hunting areas rich in rodents are needed. In the east these habitats are the fast disappearing farmlands that at one time dominated the landscape.

FACTS AND FEATURES

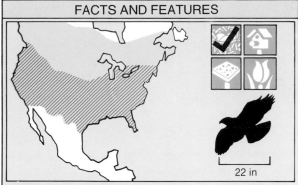

22 in

Plumage Dark head, white throat, brown back and rust colored tail. Eastern birds have a dark belly band.
Habitat Open woodlands, farmland, plains, desert regions.
Food Rodents of various kinds, snakes, lizards and rabbits.

Nest A bulky mass of sticks in a conifer or deciduous tree. In the west will build on ledges and in cacti.

The commonest large hawk of North America, the red-tailed is highly adaptable, and may be seen sitting on telegraph posts by roadsides close to towns. Although variable in plumage detail, the pink (red from above), unbarred tail readily separates this hawk. Immatures are finely streaked, lack the reddish tail, and may be confused with other species.

55

AMERICAN KESTREL *Falco sparverius*

♂

This is the smallest and commonest falcon which may be found in a variety of habitats, although it has a preference for more open areas. It frequently hovers while hunting, even by suburban highways. Very vocal when preparing to breed when the sharp, rapid kleee, kleee, kleee call may be heard. It can be enticed to breed in larger gardens by the provision of nest boxes.

THE MOST COMMON FALCON in North America, this species is found from coast to coast. Many populations are yearlong residents but major movements of northern birds can be expected in the fall. The build-up of birds in the south during the winter is remarkable.

The smallest of our falcons, the American kestrel is the only one exhibiting a russet brown back. The face is marked by two distinct black lines against a white background. A terminal band of black is present in both males and females. The males have blue-gray wings. The call is a piercing *kleeee, kleeee, kleeee;* hovering while hunting is diagnostic.

A wide variety of habitats attract this species, and as long as there is open country it can usually be found. It is at home hunting from atop a powerline pole along a busy city highway, to a ledge in a high mountain valley. In the midwest and south, birds hovering over the grasslands are a typical sight.

Kestrels feed on a wide variety of prey including small mammals, occasionally small birds, snakes and insects. During migration, dragonflies form a considerable part of their diet.

Extensive nesting box programs have shown that this species (which is a hole nester) adapts very well to man-made structures. The box used is the same in proportions to the wood duck box, being 10 in by 10 in base and 24 in high. An elliptical opening 4 in wide by 3 in high should keep out most intruding racoons. The boxes are placed in a tree at the edge of an open area. They should be secured from 20 to 40 ft up, although on rare occasions birds have occupied boxes lower down. The boxes should be protected with stain or paint and drab tones should be used—khaki and earthy tan are recommended. Place wood shavings on the floor to cradle the eggs.

FACTS AND FEATURES

11 in

Plumage Male: striped facial pattern; brown back; blue gray wing; reddish tail with terminal band. Female: foxy brown, less distinct head pattern.
Habitat Any open area. parks, farmland, prairie, desert.

Food Mainly insects (including dragonflies) small mammals, reptiles, occasionally small birds.
Nest Hole-nesting species. Takes over nest holes of woodpeckers or in natural tree or cliff cavity.

KILLDEER *Charadrius vociferus*

ALTHOUGH KNOWN AS A SHOREBIRD the killdeer is not restricted to the shoreline. It frequents ploughed fields, meadows, airfields and river valleys. However, concentrations often build up along the shore during the winter when inland areas are frozen.

The double black breast bands distinguish this species. In addition, a bright orange rump is seen when the bird is in flight. This is also the "attractant" area when the bird is approached by a predator and the bird rolls about as if with a broken wing, leading the predator away from the nest. The loud ringing *kill-deee* is a familiar sound across North America.

This species can be seen in a great variety of habitats as it walks about with erect posture in search of insects and grubs. Freshly turned over land and lawn areas after heavy rains often provide a substantial food supply.

Extensive open areas are needed to attract this bird. If fields, ploughed areas or bodies of water are nearby the chances are this species will be there. They are not shy of human habitation and have nested on flat topped buildings in the city and dodged flying golf balls while nesting on golf courses.

Two prime items needed by this species are food supply areas as outlined above and at least a small amount of water—even a wet field will do. For nesting, gravel areas are preferred. A gravelled area stands an excellent chance of attracting a nesting pair if placed near a feeding region. Two cases point this out. At a field edge a gravel area 20 ft

by 10 ft was put in to park a truck. A nesting pair was found there within one week. In the second instance, a school was built near open fields and the rear yard excavated for play. Two weeks later, killdeers nested in the yard and the following year nested on the flat roof—which was gravel covered!

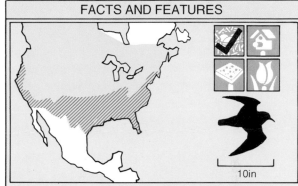

FACTS AND FEATURES

10in

Plumage Double black neck bands, soft brown above, white below, orange rump.
Habitat Inland fields, playing fields, farmlands, shoreline, sandy areas and any open area.
Food Beetles, grasshoppers, caterpillars, ants, crustaceans, invertebrates.

Nest A simple scrape in sandy soil or dirt. Little sticks added in base.

A shorebird which habitually frequents pastures, ploughed fields, airports and river valleys, the killdeer has been known to breed on roof tops and on building sites. During the breeding season, if an intruder approaches the nest or chicks, the adults will produce a broken-wing display in an effort to lead the unwanted guest away.

RING-NECKED PHEASANT *Phasianus colchicus*

♂

♀

This species was introduced for hunting. It frequents woods, hedgerows and open fields, but will venture into marshy areas in the fall and during winter months. Although retiring, it may be encouraged to venture into larger gardens by the provision of grain.

THIS SPECIES, INTRODUCED FROM ASIA, has adapted well to a variety of locations in North America, in particular the Canadian border from coast to coast. In the rich grain production areas of the midwest the species has flourished.

The ring-necked pheasant is certainly one of the best known birds because of its brilliant coloration and popularity as a game bird. The male has a rich green head offset by deep red face lappets and, in most forms, a white neck ring. The elongated tail plumes are copper colored and the body is a rich combination of coppers, greens and chestnut. The female is a tan, spotted, smaller version of the male. When flushed from cover they erupt with a startling "whir" of wings and a loud *squawk.* During the nesting season the crowing of the male is heard.

Usually seen singly or in pairs, they are not gregarious birds. They frequent a variety of habitats from farm fields, blackberry thickets and grain fields to the edges of coastal marshes. The birds may roost huddled in a ground depression or in trees. The female lays her eggs in a ground depression and escorts the young on food scratching forays well into the fall. In some areas the yearly release of game birds greatly increases the population of this species for a few months, before hunting and environmental stress bring the population back to normal levels.

In many instances where property lies near the prime pheasant habitat of weedy fields and farmlands, this species has become trained to use a feeder. They can be attracted by placing cracked corn out in regions where they have been seen. A "trail" of corn worked slowly toward the preferred feeding site will bring them into observation range. They tend to remain shy and need cover nearby to scamper into at first signs of danger. They will not come out into wide open areas with no nearby cover. Water should be provided. In many instances females have brought their young each year to such sites.

FACTS AND FEATURES

30–35 in

Plumage Large chicken like bird with long tail. Male: green head; white neck ring (in most); copper reddish body color. Female: buffy all over; no bright colors.
Habitat Farmlands, plains, brushy areas. Roosts in trees, when available.

Food Corn and grain crops are favored foods but wide variety of grass and plant seeds taken. Some small insects.
Nest Depression in grassy area or leaf edge of woodland.

NORTHERN BOBWHITE *Colinus virginianus*

ALTHOUGH A COMMON field and brushland species in the eastern half of the United States, populations in the north suffer from severe winters, and this causes a great fluctuation in numbers from year to year.

A small erect quail with short crest, the male has a bright white eye line and the female is buff. The body is a rich chestnut with black bordered white spots. The call is a diagnostic *bob---white* with uprising inflection. Also a single *hoit* is repeated year-round.

A highly gregarious species, groups feed in underbrush or field edges, scratching about for food and keeping in contact with low purring and *chuckling* notes. They scratch about for a wide variety of food and there are over 1,000 seed and fruit types listed for their diet. During the evening they roost in coveys clustered under cover for the night. During the twilight hours the piercing *hoit* of the covey call is a common sound in suitable habitats. During the breeding season the pairs separate from the covey situation.

In areas where this species abounds they can often be attracted into a feeding situation by placing grain out. A wide variety of seeds will attract—cracked corn, millet, sourgum, canary seed, peanut kernels etc. Be sure to provide cover for the birds to scamper under should a predator be in the area. Without available ready cover, the birds will not often take the chance to come out to feed. In addition, brushpiles nearby for overnight sites for the covey should enhance the chances for attracting

them. In the south, planted hedgerows along fencelines are an important habitat for this species. With proper food and cover this species can be a regular visitor to the feeding station. In the northeast, poison ivy berries are an important over-winter food source—one of the few good qualities of this plant!

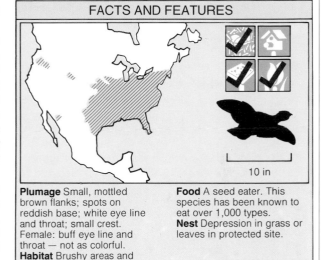

FACTS AND FEATURES

10 in

Plumage Small, mottled brown flanks; spots on reddish base; white eye line and throat; small crest. Female: buff eye line and throat — not as colorful.
Habitat Brushy areas and open woodlands with distinct understory. Weedy fields.

Food A seed eater. This species has been known to eat over 1,000 types.
Nest Depression in grass or leaves in protected site.

♂

Mainly found in the eastern half, the northern bobwhite is common in brush areas, derelict fields and open pine woods. In winter, birds come together and form coveys of up to 30 birds which, when disturbed, burst into the air together. They will visit gardens if grain is provided.

59

CALIFORNIA QUAIL *Callipepla californica*

A COMMON QUAIL of the west coast states, this species has been introduced in a number of other locations but with no great success, except for a few areas such as Utah.

A very distinctive small quail with distinct tear shaped head plume; the black face of the male is outlined in white. Gray and brown forms are distinct in different parts of the range with the color expressed in the chest and back areas. The call is a familiar sound of the west coast, being a loud three noted *one-two-three* with a rising inflection and interpreted by some as *chi-ca-go!*

Coveys of this species can be found in scrubby undergrowth, wooded ravines and valleys, woodlots and on into the weed fields of the suburbs. In each case it appears that water is a key factor in their distribution. They scuttle about the undergrowth scratching for seeds, berries and some insects. They separate into pairs during the breeding season but reunite in the fall into often extraordinary large coveys that explode from the hillsides, and glide downhill before regrouping.

Often groups will work their way into feeders if enough cover is available to allow protection from predation. A wide range of food is attractive, from cracked corn and millet to oil seed, sunflower seeds and cattle grain. Perhaps the most attractive item, however, is a water trough. This can be a simple cement indentation in the ground with running water passing through to form a pool or a depression where one can add water daily. Quail "guzzlers" are a common feature in the foothills of California and have been put out by the Game Commission to supply water for this and other quail species. Shrub piles can also attract covey formation or be used as nesting sites.

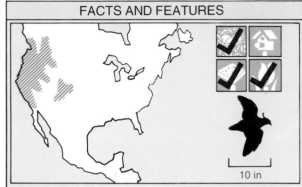

FACTS AND FEATURES

Plumage Long teardrop head — plumed in male, small in female. Black throat; scaled underparts and brown sides streaked with white.
Habitat Brushy hillsides, parkland, stream beds, open woodland with understory, chaparral.

Food Spring: tender plant leaves especially filaree and burclover. Other times: seeds of legumes.
Nest In shelter of thickets in ground depression of grass or leaves.

This species is restricted to the Western Seaboard, where it is common. It has increased in numbers in recent times, and is now found regularly in large city parks. It may be separated from the very similar Gambel's quail by its scaled belly.

♂

MOURNING DOVE *Zenaida macroura*

THIS IS THE COMMONEST and most widespread dove in the United States. It is a permanent resident throughout most of its range except the extreme northern areas around the Canadian border.

The mourning dove has a slim body with long pointed tail, pinkish brown coloration with black wing spotting and usually a dark cheek line and pink feet. In flight they rock back and forth showing upper and underwing surfaces. Their mournful call *oooh-a-oo-who who* is very often mistaken for an "owl call".

In the past 20 years this species has increased dramatically in numbers. In the weedy fields of suburban areas hundreds can be seen feeding on seeds. Backyard feeders attract large groups through the winters and farm lands are ideal locations to find them in their hundreds. When disturbed while feeding, the loud whistling of wings is an impressive sound. There are nesting records for every month of the year, even in the northern sections of its range and this aids its abundance. The nest is most often placed in an evergreen and is a sloppy jumble of a few sticks. Often the eggs can be seen from below and in many instances simply shake through the nest in high winds! Up to three clutches a year may be produced.

This species has become a standard at backyard feeders. They are fond of all sorts of bird seed with millet, oat, wheat and corn forming the bulk of their feeder diet. Plantings of thistle, buckwheat and sunflower are an attractant. Tall shrubs and evergreens near feeding sites allow roosting and nesting areas. A birdbath supplies the necessary water. Recent surveys show that two out of three feeders can now count this species as a regular visitor.

FACTS AND FEATURES

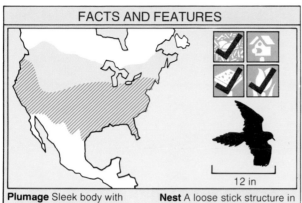

12 in

Plumage Sleek body with long tail. Warm brown with pink tint to breast.
Habitat In city parks, suburbs, feeding stations, farmlands, cultivated fields and meadows, deserts.
Food Grass seeds, grain crops preferred. Large variety of other seeds.

Nest A loose stick structure in evergreen or dense shrubbery. In cacti in desert areas.

Common and widespread, this long-tailed dove has increased dramatically thanks to weedy urban fringes and feeding tables. It may be found nesting in all but the most northerly areas, in all months of the year. The nest is a flimsy structure of twigs upon which the two whitish eggs are placed.

COMMON GROUND DOVE *Columbina passerina*

A FAIRLY COMMON BIRD of the Gulf Coast, throughout Florida and on into the extreme southern states, this species is also common in southern Texas and the extreme southwest. Indications are that the population is slowly extending northward.

A small stocky dove with a distinctive short tail, it has scale-like markings on the head and upper breast. In flight, the bright red of the primaries is easily seen even though the wings are a whirring blur. It often jumps from cover, flies a short way then plunges back to the ground and scampers off.

They prefer brushy areas and open ground with nearby cover. During the breeding season they pair off, but the rest of the year is spent in groups. Perched in low shrubs their mellow *who---up* call is a familiar sound throughout their range.

Though fairly shy, in most instances, the birds will move into a backyard if shrubby cover is provided. In order to attract them, it is best to place various grains (shelled oats, millet, canary seed) under the cover they frequent, rather than out in the open. In more open country they can be attracted by proper planting of fence lines. Various composites rich with seeds, cacti (to supress predators and weeds) and grasses should be allowed to remain, and the doves will find all they need to establish themselves. If vegetation is left in place along the fence line be sure to use metal fence posts or alternate metal and wood posts to make sure the fence survives should fire reach the area. Water should be provided in the vicinity in the form of a bird bath or small pool.

This common ground dove is a bird of the far south, but it is apparently extending its range northward. It resembles a small mourning dove on the ground, but is distinguished by its shorter tail. Its flight is a very rapid and short-lived one, during which rufous patches may be seen. It prefers open areas with low scrub, and although shy, may be attracted into backyards, if low cover and various seeds are provided. The nest is usually placed on the ground.

FACTS AND FEATURES

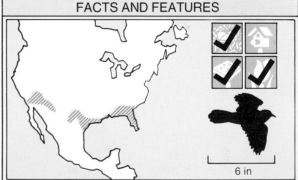

6 in

Plumage Small, short tailed dove. Brown back, gray on head; scaled head and breast. Rusty primaries in flight.
Habitat Weedy areas, field edges, hedgerows, cultivated land, cactus thickets, brushy rangeland.

Food Mainly seeds of grasses and forbs such as doveweed. May take some insects.
Nest Frail platform of sticks on ground or in shrub or low tree.

GREAT HORNED OWL *Bubo virginianus*

THIS LARGE OWL, found throughout the United States, is unmistakable with its large, wide-set "ear" tufts, orange facial disks and dark brown plumage. Its call, familiar in the twilight of winter is a deep-tone series of five hoots.

A very adapatable owl, the great horned owl lives in a wide variety of habitats—from deep forests to city parks. They take advantage of other birds' nests which may be on cliff faces, in trees or large cacti. In many instances the eggs are placed in the concavity of a broken snag. Occasionally they will also nest directly on the ground. A wide variety of prey is taken including birds and mammals. Prey up to the size of skunks and grouse are brought back to the nest. As with all owls, their nocturnal habits often belie their presence. However, the pellets of undigested food that are regurgitated and fecal material often give away their roosts and nest sites. They are very defensive of their nest sites, and caution should be displayed when approaching any young that may be on the ground or low in a tree or bush.

The young are raised through the summer months and they then disperse. During this period they show up in the middle of cities, on rooftops etc., so the chance of an encounter is increased. (One bird spent two months in an open press box of a football stadium in mid-winter!) If a substantial grove of trees or other suitable habitat is nearby there is a chance that the birds will nest. The chances of their nesting can be increased if you take sticks up into substantial crotches of trees and make a platform that looks like an old crow's nest or flattened hawk's nest. In the east, the owls sometimes move in by mid-February.

Largest of the owls with "ear" tufts, the great horned can be found in many situations from dense forests to city parks. Like most owls, it is more often heard than seen. The call is made up of deep hoots which are more commonly heard during the late winter. May be confused with the smaller, long-eared owl, but its broader head, wider spaced "ear" tufts and barred underparts should distinguish it.

FACTS AND FEATURES

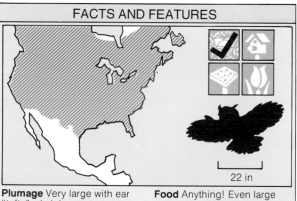

22 in

Plumage Very large with ear "tufts"; dark brown to tawny. Orange face disks; barred below; white throat.
Habitat All types: from deep forest to desert, open woodlands, inner city parks, cliffs, canyons and wooded thickets.

Food Anything! Even large mammals as big as skunks. Rats, squirrels, grouse, even weasles, snakes and insects.
Nest In modified nest of crow, hawk or heron but at times on cliff faces or in ground depression.

EASTERN SCREECH OWL *Otus asio*

THIS SPECIES IS FOUND from eastern Montana south through most of Texas on through to the east coast. A recent separation from the western screech owl *(Otus kennicotti)* makes definition of the western edge of the range difficult.

Perhaps one of the best known of all owls, its small size, feather ear tufts and camouflage coloration is the stereotyped image of what most people think an owl should look like.

There are two distinct color phases. One a rusty red, the other a gray. Intermediate birds of a brownish tint will also be encountered. The call consists of a quavering whistle and a hollow trill. Several other barks, whines and reverberations can also be produced but they are not the norm.

Certainly the commonest owl in the eastern half of the United States, it has adapted well to live with spreading populations. They can inhabit parks, orchards, backyards, gardens as well as woodlands. The nest is placed in a hollow cavity and other cavities are used as roosting sites. Strictly nocturnal, a roost close to the trunk of a tree may be discovered in the daytime or birds may be seen taking in the early morning sun at a cavity opening. During the breeding season some birds even call in the daytime.

If these diminutive owls are suspected to be in the area, if they have been heard calling, or if there seems to be a suitable habitat, the erection of a nesting box may attract them, if not to nest, perhaps at least to day roost. Any large box will do from the size used by a flicker up to wood duck size. Hence a base of 8 to 10 in square and sides from 15 to 20 in will suffice. The opening should be at least 3 in in diameter. Place a layer of sawdust inside to protect any eggs. These boxes should be placed in an open wood or facing a field. Running water appears to be a prerequisite of prime habitat.

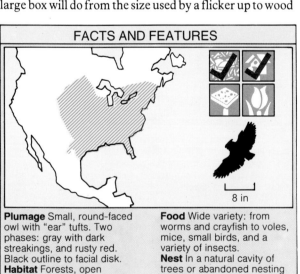

FACTS AND FEATURES

8 in

Plumage Small, round-faced owl with "ear" tufts. Two phases: gray with dark streakings, and rusty red. Black outline to facial disk.
Habitat Forests, open woodlands, swamps, river areas, parks. Wherever there are trees!

Food Wide variety: from worms and crayfish to voles, mice, small birds, and a variety of insects.
Nest In a natural cavity of trees or abandoned nesting hole of another species. Rarely, one will lay in an old squirrel nest!

The commonest, small, "eared" owl of towns and wooded areas, the eastern screech owl has three color phases including a gray, brown and rusty form. It can be encouraged to take up residence by the provision of nest boxes in which it may either roost or breed. Boxes should be placed high in trees, preferably close to a running stream.

BARN OWL *Tyto alba*

A FAIRLY COMMON OWL throughout its range this species is found over most of the United States outside the extreme northern part of the midwest. Markedly more common in the southern part of its range, in the northern regions they seem to go through good years followed by periods of low numbers, then build up again. This is one of the few species found throughout the world.

A very pale bird with golden back and wings, its heartlike face is outlined with a dark band. The flight is very bouyant, and it hunts in open country, never woodland. The call is a loud, whistling hiss.

Of all the owls this species has best adapted to life near human habitation. It is the only owl frequently to take up residence in the city in abandoned buildings and hunt rats in dark alleyways undetected by the residents in the area. Though they will nest in natural tree cavities and on sheer cliff ledges, they also occupy farm buildings, railway tressels, old water towers, church towers and the like. They will also take over duck boxes in open marshlands. Nesting is based on available food hence there are nest records for every month of the year. Up to 10 eggs have been found in a nest but rarely do more than six young survive. A bird of the low light hours of dawn and dusk, they can often be seen hunting at dump edges, open meadows and marsh edges and then carrying food back to the nest site. They hunt through the night.

If barn owls have been seen in your area, or if the habitat seems right, the best attractant is a nest box or nest ledge. A nest box on the lines of a wood duck box 10 in square at the base and 2 ft high with a 4 in wide by 3 in high hole is sufficient. A simple, open top wooden box 2 ft square with one side cut to the halfway point leaving a high lip for egg protection works very well. These boxes can be fixed to high posts, inside likely buildings (for example high in the rafters of a barn or building loft), but be sure there is always an opening left into the building so the owls can come and go at will. Boxes have been placed directly on the sides of houses up near the highest peak.

FACTS AND FEATURES

16 in

Plumage Medium size owl with golden gray coloration. White underparts; heart-shaped face edged with brown; small eyes.
Habitat Mainly in open areas; cultivated land, farmland, parks, inner city areas. Usually near human habitation.

Food Rodents (voles, mice, rats).
Nest Abandoned buildings, barns, hollow trees, animal burrows, holes in sand banks. The most adaptable of owls.

At night, the ghostly, apparently all white, silhouette of this owl may be picked up in car headlights as it hunts for prey. It particularly likes marshy areas to hunt, and may be seen during the twilight hours. It is well adapted to living in close proximity to man; it will utilize disused buildings, barns and church towers.

CHIMNEY SWIFT *Chaetura pelagica*

FOUND FROM SOUTHEAST CANADA south through Texas, the chimney swift is the only swift seen consistently within this range.

In flight it looks like a "cigar with wings." The wings are held stiffly and beat rapidly, the tail is square when fanned out. The call is a loud twittering especially when in flocks. During the breeding season this species performs a rocking display with wings held high over its back, and twists and turns in flight as it plunges downward. It feeds only on the wing, collects nesting material on the wing and mates on the wing! Often it feeds through the night and is suspected of sleeping while in flight!

Commonest within the cities but also found in the countryside, it has a particular predilection for nesting in chimneys and has also been found nesting in building lofts, barn silos and inside hollow trees.

The nest is a crossthatch of small sticks, glued together with saliva and placed in the corner or recess of adjoining walls or structures. The birds cling to these walls with their small feet propped up by the stiffened bristles of their tail. Spectacular masses can be seen entering chimneys on occasions to roost and nest. During these mass gatherings a darkening funnel of birds is often seen, twittering loudly, then quickly disappearing from sight as they fly into the chimney for the night.

Unless there is an unused chimney, or hollow tree of some size in the area, the most likely encounters with this species will be seeing their flight displays overhead or seeing them hawking through gardens for insects. If a large body of water is close by they often swoop over the surface to scoop up water or actually splash into it, bathing for the second or two of contact. In many instances, small cabin chimneys or the chimneys of city homes have been used by a pair of these birds. After such a visit, the nest should be cleaned out before the chimney is re-used. The birds would not re-use the nest the next year but would re-build it in any event.

FACTS AND FEATURES

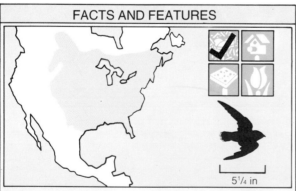

5¼ in

Plumage Cigar-shaped body with long pointed wings. Uniform gray/brown color. Pale near throat.
Habitat May appear overhead on the wing anywhere within its range (ie over forest, city etc).
Food Flying insects. Feeds only on the wing. May feed all night.

Nest A crossthatch of twigs collected in flight, and glued together with saliva. In chimney, rock face or natural tree cavity.

This swift is the one most likely to be encountered east of the Missouri and Mississippi rivers. It is normally seen and heard in noisy flocks. On migration, they often roost in large numbers in chimneys, usually entering the site in a characteristic funnel formation at sunset.

RUBY-THROATED HUMMINGBIRD *Archilochus colubris*

This is the only hummer commonly found east of the Mississippi, where it frequents edges of woodland, gardens and boggy areas. It can be attracted by tubular flowers, or by feeders containing a sugar solution. Females lack the red throat of the male.

THIS IS THE ONLY HUMMINGBIRD found east of the Mississippi river. A few western species may occur within this area from time to time but they are not resident. This species has the most extensive range of any North American hummingbird, and even goes through the southern part of Canada.

The diminutive size and "blurr" of wings makes it impossible to confuse this bird with any other. However, there is a group of moths that look similar and visit flowers but these are smaller and have transparent wings. As the name indicates the throat is a reflective red and the underparts a grayish white. The head and back are metallic green with a black line to the eye. Females lack the red throat. The sound produced is a high smacking twitter. From the side, the red throat may appear blackish.

A common bird throughout most of its range, it is constantly on the move searching out tubular flowers to feed at. During the night it reduces its body functions and goes into a torpor state so as to reduce metabolism and the need to feed constantly. The preferred habitats are at the edges of clearings, woodlots, over roads, in gardens, and a favored spot in the northeast in bogs. The nest is a tiny plant fiber cup, covered with lichens and balanced on a limb. They are on average 3 inches across!

The normal clutch is two young. During migration numbers can be seen in the patches of fall flowers such as *Impatiens* (touch me not) as they migrate to the Gulf Coast and then on to Central America.

Masses of flowers will attract passing birds or hummingbirds nesting nearby. Any tubular types of flowers will do. The trumpet creeper is just such a plant, and the large orange trumpets are a favored feeding flower. Honeysuckles (of the 10 or so common garden species) are ideal.

Hummingbird feeders can also be placed out. These can be purchased or made simply. A hamster water bottle forms the basis. Cut a large flower shape out of aluminum and paint it bright red. A hole in the center allows insertion of the water bottle tube. Sugar water tinted with red food coloring is a sure attractant. Care should be taken as honeybees also often use these feeders. In some instances strings of these feeders on a porch have attracted 20 or more of these hummingbirds.

FACTS AND FEATURES

3¾ in

Plumage Small, fast-moving bird. Green above and white below. Reflective red throat in male (streaked with white in female).
Habitat Gardens, open woodlands and boggy areas.
Food Nectar of flowers, but will also take tree sap and some insects.

Nest A beautiful plant fiber cup, covered with lichens in coniferous or deciduous tree. Usually out near branch tip.

ANNA'S HUMMINGBIRD *Calypte anna*

A COMMON RESIDENT of the extreme west coast, this species ranges across southern California and on into Arizona.

It is the only North American hummingbird with a red iridescent top to its head. The throat gorget is large and a brilliant red. The back and under-belly are green and the bill is relatively short. Females though green on the back and dusky gray below, have a variable amount of red streaking and spots in the throat area. Males are fairly "vocal", often "singing" from a treetop perch. The "song" is a jumble of squeaky notes and chips.

This is a very common bird throughout most of its range and can be found in gardens, woodlots, and scrubby areas in the mountain and desert regions. As they dart about the loud *chit-chit-chit* of their call attracts attention. During the breeding season they perform a pendulum dance, as do so many of the other hummingbirds. In this case a vertical flight is executed followed by a low arc at the base, which if drawn out would resemble a backward J.

Tubular flowers of any sort are sure to attract this species. Flower gardens and even porch hangings will have their share of visitors. Red flowers appear to be the preferred color. Trumpet creepers, flame vines, fuschias and the like are real favorites.

Hummingbird feeders either purchased or made (*see* 'Ruby-throated') can be the center of activity in a backyard. In many instances a yard offering such facilities will also be the site of the tightly woven plant fiber lined nest placed astride a branch.

Restricted to the Western Seaboard where it is the only hummer with a song which is delivered from a perch. Females have only a few red spots on the mainly white throat; the tail is green and tipped white. This sex may be confused with that of the black-chinned, but it is larger and more heavily built.

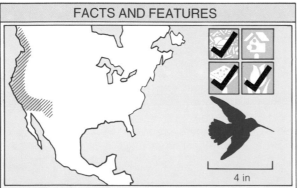

FACTS AND FEATURES

4 in

Plumage Metallic green above, a white to grayish white below. Male has red forehead and throat feathers that wrap nearly to back of neck, a brilliant red.
Habitat Open woodlands, chaparral, hillsides, gardens.
Food Mainly flower nectar but will take insects and sap from open tree wounds.

Nest A small cup on a low limb in thicket made of down, mosses and covered with cobwebs.

BLACK-CHINNED HUMMINGBIRD *Archilochus alexandri*

♂

A common hummer of the western mountains, this bird is the only North American species with a truely black throat. Females are hard to separate from Costa's in the more southern areas of their range, but may be separated from Anna's by their smaller, less plump size. They often catch insects in the manner of flycatchers.

THE MOST WIDESPREAD of the western hummingbirds, this species ranges from central Texas on a diagonal to western Washington through to the west coast. It does not occur in the high mountains.

A small hummingbird, it is metallic green above and on the sides, and the male has a black throat bordered with purple on the lower portion. The female is green backed, whitish below with grayish sides and tends to have a tannish white forehead with slight green throat streaks.

A common bird of the lowlands, coastal regions and to some extent of the lower flanks of the mountains, it can be seen in gardens, scrub lots and many man-made areas. With the abundance of tubular flowers in the west, the hummingbirds have radiated in considerable numbers. The nest is a fiber cup covered with cobwebs and placed in shrub or lower tree limbs. During courtship, they display by flying back and forth in a shallow arc called the "pendulum display."

As with all the hummingbirds, flowers are the main means of attracting them. Tubular flowers are very important for feeding. Plants of tree tobacco are often an attraction for groups of these birds. Coral flowers, filias, penstamens, monkey flowers and the like can also be attractions. Honeysuckles are particularly well liked. In addition, hummingbird feeders can be purchased or made (*see* "Ruby-throated"). So abundant are the hummingbirds in the west, that large feeders such as

gallon chicken waterers are used. In some notable locations where hummingbird feeding has gone on for some time a hundred or more birds can be seen in the air at one time! Restaurants often have strings of feeders out, so patrons can watch the birds' antics while dining.

FACTS AND FEATURES

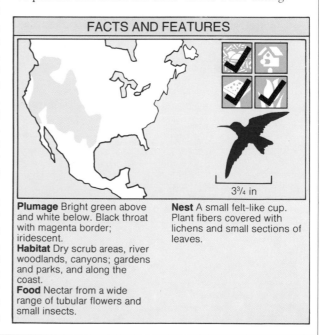

3¾ in

Plumage Bright green above and white below. Black throat with magenta border; iridescent.
Habitat Dry scrub areas, river woodlands, canyons; gardens and parks, and along the coast.
Food Nectar from a wide range of tubular flowers and small insects.

Nest A small felt-like cup. Plant fibers covered with lichens and small sections of leaves.

69

RED-HEADED WOODPECKER *Melanerpes erythrocephalus*

THIS SPECIES RANGES THROUGHOUT the central and eastern portion of the United States, but is missing from the extreme southern tips of Florida and Texas, and northern New England.

The male and female are colored alike with a brilliant red head contrasting with the black and white body. The underparts are pure white and the black of the back, wings and tail are accentuated by a white rump and large white wing patches. Immature birds are brown where adults are black, and have a brown hood and faint brown chest streaks.

This is a bird of the open areas with a marked preference for farmlands, open pine woods and woodlot edges, parks and orchards. Its habit of dipping low to the ground when leaving a perch such as a roadside fence post, has spelled doom for many a bird along a highway.

The ideal site for nesting is a large dead tree on the edge of a field or open area.

Direct competition with the European starling has forced this species away from many of its former haunts. Modification of habitat has also applied pressure within the shrinking range of this bird. Populations appear to undergo periodic rises and falls and after long periods of absence the species may reappear at nests in old sites. It is the dominant woodpecker in its territory and will actively defend its "territory" from all other woodpecker species. It also defends a winter territory in which it has hidden acorns, nuts and berries that will form the bulk of its winter larder.

Should a bird or pair be in residence in your area several approaches can be taken to keep them in residence. Be sure that any favored nesting sites such as large trees are not removed. If adequate seeds and suet are placed out, especially in the winter, the birds will usually start making daily visits—some birds may even overwinter at feeders. Nesting boxes on occasion will attract them but they prefer natural cavities. A large box is most suitable—6 in square on the bottom, 15 in high with a 2 in diameter hole 8 in from the floor. This box can be placed from 6 to 15 ft up in a tree but be sure it is on the edge of an opening such as extensive lawns, a field or open woodlot. Sawdust should be put in the bottom for the egg surface. Fruit placed in tree crotches will also attract their attention. Control of starlings at a feeding station by means of special feeders will also increase the chance of nesting.

Although the range covers much of the central and eastern halves of the United States, the species is far from common. Competition with the European Starling for nesting holes, and its habit of swooping low over roads has helped to reduce its numbers in many parts of its range.

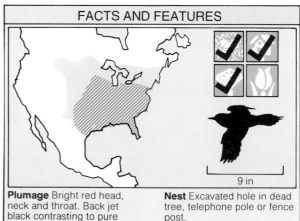

FACTS AND FEATURES

9 in

Plumage Bright red head, neck and throat. Back jet black contrasting to pure white underparts. Large white patches in the wing.

Habitat Open forests, farmlands, parks, swamplands.

Food Acorns, wild berries, fruits and other nuts. Insects, and other small invertebrates.

Nest Excavated hole in dead tree, telephone pole or fence post.

RED-BELLIED WOODPECKER *Melanerpes carolinus*

ALREADY RANGING FROM CENTRAL TEXAS, north to Missouri and eastward to the coast, this species is expanding northward slowly each year and is now found with regularity in Massachusetts during the summer. In the winter they withdraw from the northernmost part of the range and move down from the highest part of the Appalachians.

A zebra striped back and white rump with a red top on the head is the distinguising mark. In the male the red runs from the nape of the neck over the crown to the bill base. In the female the forecrown is grey with the red concentrated on the back of the head. The name "red-bellied" refers to a light wash of orange-red on the lower belly feathers which is often very difficult to distinguish. In flight, large white patches are visible near the wing tips.

This is a very loud bird and its raucous *churring* notes often give its presence away before it is seen. It forages on limbs in normal woodpecker fashion but also spends a good deal of time on the ground feeding on seeds, nuts, berries and the like. Insects are also excavated from the ground. Aggressive, it may dominate downy and hairy woodpeckers in its area, but many tame readily, and allow a close approach. It can be found in a great variety of habitats from the garden and woodlot to swamplands, pine woods and orchards. In the northern part of its range it has made its greatest inroads in the oak woodlands, the acorn being a favored food. The nest hole is excavated from 10 to 30 ft up in a wide variety of trees from palms to pines.

This is a species of the eastern states which is gradually expanding its range. It has adapted to city living well, for it will readily use nest boxes. It is extremely vocal and the raucous churring *call often betrays its presence long before it is seen.*

FACTS AND FEATURES

9¼ in

Plumage Ladder back; red to top of head and nape. Tan forehead in female. Underparts tan; light red tint to belly.
Habitat Forest, palm woods, pine woods, orchards, suburban and city areas. In northeast prefers oak woodland.

Food Acorns, and various other tree fruit; many insect species.
Nest Excavated hole in living or dead deciduous or palm tree.

This species has adapted well to living in the city as well as the suburbs. They will excavate a telephone pole along a city street or a tree right next to a house. Nesting boxes placed out are an attraction but natural cavities are preferred. They come readily to feeding stations and take a wide variety of food, from oil seed, sunflowers, seeds, cracked corn and oats right down to the small millets. A suet bag suspended from a tree will also get a lot of attention, especially in the winter months. Fruit such as oranges, cut in half and laid on the ground, wedged in tree crotches or impaled on pegs from a board will also be eaten enthusiastically.

DOWNY WOODPECKER *Picoides pubescens*

THIS SPECIES RANGES THOUGHOUT the contiguous states except for the southwestern region of the lower section of New Mexico, Arizona and the Rio Grande Valley of Texas. It is found in the north through Canada and on into Alaska.

This is the best known of all the woodpeckers in North America. Looking like a miniature hairy woodpecker, it is white below, with white spots in the black wings and a white back. However, the outer tail feathers are white spotted with black. The male sports a solid red patch on the back of the head. The call is a loud *pick* and a rapid down slurring, rattling call.

It is found virtually everywhere there are trees! City parks, orchards, woodlots, deep woods and even corn fields. Rather tame, they tend to climb higher in the tree as a human approaches rather than fly off. If other birds are scolding, the downy is quick to respond and to come to investigate.

Downies will come to feeding stations readily for seeds and suet. No special requirements are needed. They will come to a feeder shelf, cling to hanging feeders and investigate peanut butter smeared into pine cones and sprinkled with seeds. Inquisitiveness seems to run in the species and in most instances any type of feeder will be investigated. They will readily accept bird houses erected for them. A small house with a 4 in square base and 10 in or so in height will suit them well. The hole needs to be 1¼ in in diameter and placed 7 in above the floor to cradle the eggs. The house can be placed on a post or tree about 10 ft off the ground. In areas where land clearance is underway, old trees that are knocked down can provide suitable nesting "boxes." Remove an adequate section that contains an old excavation from the felled tree and strap this to a tree in your yard. In many cases this will be readily accepted.

The downy is the smallest woodpecker, not much larger than a sparrow, which is found commonly almost throughout the United States. It has managed to maintain its numbers in urban areas where it is found in parks, gardens and orchards. It will readily use nest boxes.

FACTS AND FEATURES

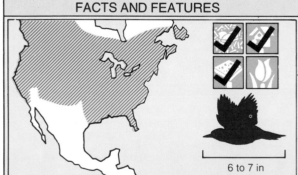

6 to 7 in

Plumage Small black and white woodpecker. White back; outer tail feathers white with black spots; black cheek patch. Male has red patch at back of head.
Habitat Open mixed forests, orchards, parks, city yards and suburbs.

Food Ninety percent insect forms, of which wood boring beetles make up a large part. Also some berries and seeds.
Nest Excavated hole in dead trees or stumps often low to ground.

HAIRY WOODPECKER *Picoides villosus*

This bird is most likely to be confused with the smaller, downy, and black-backed, three-toed woodpecker. It is separated from the former by its larger bill, and from the latter by its unmarked flanks and red patch on the back of the head.

WIDESPREAD THROUGHOUT THE UNITED STATES, Canada and on into Alaska, this species and the downy are the backyard woodpeckers of the country.

A medium sized woodpecker, it is easily identified by its white underparts, dark upperparts with spotting on the wings and a white back. The outer tail feathers are pure white compared to the spotted feathers of the smaller look-alike downy. The male has a red patch on the back of the head divided by a thin black line.

A wide range of habitats is frequented by the hairy woodpecker—deep woods, woodlots, orchards, city parks and backyards. The loud single *peak* note or rapid tapping is often a giveaway that one is present. Once a favored tree with insect infections is located, it will spend weeks making frequent visits, stripping the limbs bare in search of food. The nest is a cavity in a dead tree.

Because of its abundance and adaptability to habitation, this is one bird that will be among the first to show up at a feeding station. Occasionally it will take seeds scattered on the ground or in a ledge feeder. The main attraction is often suet placed in some form of holder. In the summer this can quickly become rancid and during this time the species is off raising young with plenty of "wild" food available. But during the winter months daily visits to the suet is guaranteed. They also use nesting boxes placed out for them. A 6 in square base,

15 in high and with a $1^{1}/_{2}$ in hole placed 11 in up will do the trick. Place sawdust on the floor for the eggs. The box should be placed above 10 ft off the ground either on a post or directly on a tree.

FACTS AND FEATURES

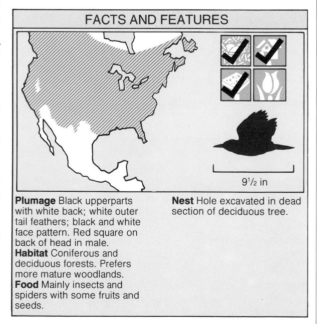

9½ in

Plumage Black upperparts with white back; white outer tail feathers; black and white face pattern. Red square on back of head in male.
Habitat Coniferous and deciduous forests. Prefers more mature woodlands.
Food Mainly insects and spiders with some fruits and seeds.

Nest Hole excavated in dead section of deciduous tree.

73

NORTHERN FLICKER *Colaptes auratus*

Unlike other woodpeckers, the flicker spends much of its time on the ground in search of its favorite food, ants. When disturbed from this position, it shows its characteristic white rump as it flies away.

♂

THIS IS A COMMON SPECIES throughout the United States and on through Canada into Alaska.

It is a large brown woodpecker with a barred back and conspicuous white rump seen best when it takes off from the ground. It has spotted underparts and no white wing patches. Three forms occur. The "yellow-shafted" with yellow shafts to wing feathers and a black mushtache mark in the male and with a distinct red patch on the back of the head. The "red-shafted" form has salmon red feather shafts in the wing and a red mustache mark in the male. The third color form is found only in the southwest and has wing shafts of yellow but a red mustache in the male. In the past this was known under the name of the "gilded flicker."

Of all the woodpeckers, this species spends the most time on the ground, foraging for ants. The loud ringing *yuck, yuck, yuck* is a familiar sound from coast to coast. The nest is placed in a dead snag and takes several days to excavate. In suburban and city areas this species is often evicted by starlings who wait until the work is complete! The guilded "race" in the southwest excavates its home in the giant saguaro cacti. The loud rapping to set off the territories, the bobbing antics of males occupying the same area and challenging each other, and the loud ringing calls make it one of the best known of the woodpeckers. Walking across open areas the flash of white from the rump is a most familiar site.

This species frequents a wide range of habitats, and there are almost certainly birds living in your area. In general they are not attracted to feeding station areas unless pressed for food. When they do visit, suet and sunflower seeds seem to be preferred. You can place out nesting boxes for them with success. The nest box should have a 7 in square base and be about 18 in high. The $2^{1}/_{2}$ in hole should be located 14 in above the floor. This box can be placed in a post or side of a tree 8 to 20 ft above the ground. Place a considerable amount of sawdust in the base (4 in or so) to duplicate the floor of a natural excavation. Face the opening out over an open area.

FACTS AND FEATURES

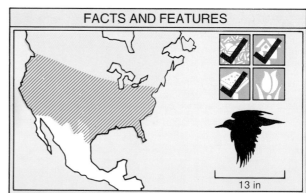

13 in

Plumage Large, brown backed with barring; white rump; spotted underparts; no wing patches.
Habitat Open woodlands, field edges, parks, orchards, city areas. Often feeds on ground. Some forms in desert.

Food Fifty percent of its diet consists of ants; also takes other insects and berries.
Nest Excavated hole in deciduous tree. Gilded race nests in large cacti.

EASTERN PHOEBE *Sayornis phoebe*

A SUMMER RESIDENT over the eastern half of the United States and all but the far north of Canada, this species winters in the southern states, in particular along the Gulf Coast and Florida. Strays occasionally reach the west coast especially in the winter.

The Eastern Phoebe is a brownish gray bird with dark gray head, black bill and pale underparts usually with a significant grayish olive tint. Fall birds in fresh plumage show a marked yellowish cast and young birds can appear to have two wing bars. A typical posture is rather upright on a limb with the tail flicked slowly up and down. There is no eye ring. The call is a rapid *fee—beep* that can be given in a sequence that is up and down in inflection. Many people mistake the drawn out mating call of the black-capped chickadee, *feeee–beeeee,* for this species.

Widespread in its habitat preferences, it can be found in city parks, farms, orchards on through to deep woodlands. The large plant fiber and moss cup nest is placed in a diverse number of locations—under bridges, roadside culverts, exposed building rafters and eves. In woodlands it may place the nest on the wall of a large tree cavity or rocky ledge of a cliff face. During the summer it is an exclusive insectivore but it changes in the fall when berries are often ingested. This allows some birds to stay on into early winter in the north and on rare occasions through the winter!

Although they will not come to a feeder, they will almost certainly pass through your grounds in spring and fall movements, or take up residence through the year in the southern sections. With water nearby, a steady insect supply is usually assured and can be an attractant. In addition they often accept nesting platforms placed out for them. These should have at least 6 in square bases with a slight lip around the edge to aid in nest protection. If it is to be placed in a fairly open area a roof should be added for weather protection. However, if the shelf is placed under a roof overhang such a roof is not needed. Most flat surfaces will be checked early in the year for possible nest sites, so if taken indoors for the winter they need to be put out early (by mid-March in the northern sections of the range).

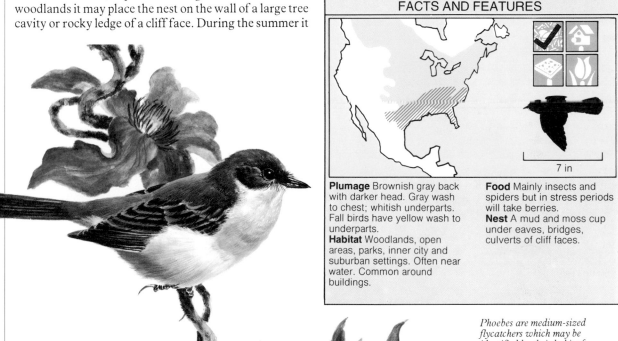

FACTS AND FEATURES

Plumage Brownish gray back with darker head. Gray wash to chest; whitish underparts. Fall birds have yellow wash to underparts.
Habitat Woodlands, open areas, parks, inner city and suburban settings. Often near water. Common around buildings.

Food Mainly insects and spiders but in stress periods will take berries.
Nest A mud and moss cup under eaves, bridges, culverts of cliff faces.

7 in

Phoebes are medium-sized flycatchers which may be identified by their habit of leisurely jerking their tails downward. Lack of wing bars easily separate adults from other flycatchers, but immatures do possess them and are easily confused.

EASTERN KINGBIRD *Tyrannus tyrannus*

THE EASTERN KINGBIRD IS WIDESPREAD in its distribution and is found from the far west (just short of California and Arizona) through to the east coast and throughout most of Canada.

A slaty gray bird with a darker head, it has white underparts and a dark tail with a white terminal band. The male has a red crown.

This bird often sits on tops of bushes or trees from which it may venture to catch large passing insects, or to chase away intruding bird species. On seizing the prey, the bill is snapped shut with an audible click. Very adaptable, this species will occupy many types of habitat, but to encourage breeding, the provision of a pond appears necessary.

One of the most typical movements of the bird is to dart from a treetop position and fly about with rapid shallow wingbeats giving off loud *twittering* notes. It also darts out from treetops to secure winged insects. Known for its pugnacity, it defends its territory against most intruders and has been seen diving and harrassing passing bald eagles!

A bird of open areas, orchards are favored spots as well as city parks, backyards, farmlands and woodlots. In most instances water is a key factor in selecting nesting areas. The nest is a rather bulky affair placed in a crotch of a large tree in the area. This species is most active in the evening when insects rise over fields or nearby water. They are also known for their love of honeybees and many a wild bee colony has a resident pair of kingbirds near by.

Due to its wide distribution and adaptability to so many environments, there is a good chance that a pair of these birds will be in residence anywhere you live within their range.

Flowers usually mean insects and therefore can be an attractant for kingbirds. If water is available in the form of a pool, pond or stream the species may nest. As an inducement to nesting, material can be placed out to aid in nest building. Favored items are feathers and string. Feathers can also be scattered on the ground near the nest site and string draped on the lower limbs of trees. Be sure the string is not too long so as to cause entanglement when picked up by the birds. Lengths of 4 in or so will be long enough.

FACTS AND FEATURES

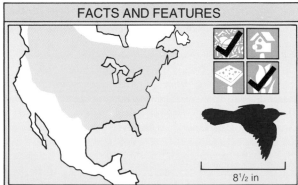

8½ in

Plumage Gray back; dark head; white underparts. Dark tail with white terminal band.
Habitat Open areas, parks, orchards, bogs, farmlands. Often near water.
Food All forms of winged insects; enjoys bees. Will occasionally take berries.

Nest Large cup of grasses, weeds and other plant material, lined with plant down. Usually high up in tree crotch.

LEAST FLYCATCHER *Empidonax minimus*

A common bird of scrub areas, wood margins and unkept orchards of the eastern states. It is the smallest of the Empidonax *flycatchers, which are almost impossible to identify from their plumage alone. This species is best separated by its song, which consists of a dry* che-bek, *repeated 50-70 times a minute.*

THIS SPECIES IS WIDESPREAD in the northeast and on into Canada, and during migration is a common bird north from Texas.

A member of the famous *Empidonax* group, this is the smallest and commonest of these drab flycatchers to be seen in the east. Grayish in appearance, with distinct wing bars and a white eye ring, it often bobs its tail while sitting. The call is as good a field mark as any—a rapid *chee-bik, chee-bik* that is repeated endlessly.

The least flycatcher is a bird of open areas as well as open forests. During migration it is likely to be found just about anywhere—orchards, backyards, parks and indeed any locality with insects. The nest is a small cup of plant fibers covered with plant material and cobwebs. This is placed astride a tree limb and is often very difficult to locate as it looks like just another lump on the limb.

This species is not easy to attract with food or housing, but if there are open areas nearby with plots of trees this is an ideal situation for nesting. Extensive flower planting will also ensure a significant insect population, which is sure to attract these birds.

FACTS AND FEATURES

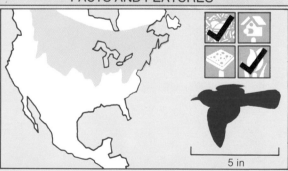

5 in

Plumage Small bird with large head; gray olive above; gray tinted underparts. Distinct eye ring and wing bars.
Habitat Open woodlands, swampy areas, orchards, parkland.
Food Almost exclusively insect matter and spiders.

Nest A well made, deep cup of plant fibers, bark and grasses. Lined with down and fibers. Looks similar to limb it is placed on.

PURPLE MARTIN *Progne subis*

THE RANGE FOR THIS SPECIES shows a division in the lower 48 states. An eastern population ranges from the east coast (Maine to Florida) west to mid North Dakota and central southern Canada and on a straight line south through central Texas. A small population can also be found in central Montana. The western area runs in a narrow strip from Washington to southern California, with pockets in Utah and Arizona.

It is the largest of the swallows in North America. The male is a shimmering bluish purple all over, the female pale gray below and brown backed.

This large swallow has become a favorite of the backyard birdwatchers. Historically they nested in large tree cavities and old woodpecker holes. Though they still nest in these places in mountain areas, they have adapted very well to especially constructed communal nesting boxes. These elaborate homes often allow 30 or so pairs to nest. In some regions hollow gourds are put out for the birds to nest in. They are especially grown gourds that must be left outside until the killing frost. This causes the outside to rot away and once this material is scraped off the solid inner layer will harden. A coat of shellac will add protection. Hung in clusters these gourds serve the same purpose as the large houses.

Special requirements seem to be needed to attract a colony of these birds. Apart from proper housing and water nearby, an extensive open area, such as fields, afford the bird what is termed a "swoop" zone before entering the house. In addition it is an excellent foraging area. An additional attractant for the bird is crushed egg shells placed near the nesting site. They will quickly discover these and spend considerable time feeding on them and carrying them up to the female birds during their courtship periods.

Nesting boxes should be removed in the fall for cleaning. They should be erected in early March in the northern areas and mid-February in the south. This will allow the first "scouts," that arrive before the main flocks, to locate proper quarters. They should not be left up year-round as starlings and house sparrows will invade the nest before the scouts arrive.

The birds' diet is almost exclusively insects with mosquitoes forming a substantial part of it.

♀

♂

Purple martins can be enticed into the garden by multicelled nesting boxes or gourds. Males are unmistakable — all dark with areas of purple iridescence. Females and young birds can be confused with other swallows, but they are larger and have broader wings. They regularly form large roosting flocks in late summer, even within city limits.

FACTS AND FEATURES

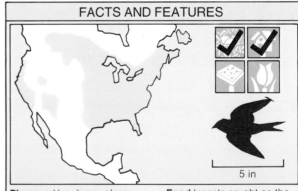

5 in

Plumage Very large, glossy metallic blue. Female gray brown below.
Habitat Open woodlands, clear cut areas, farmlands near lake edges, saguaro deserts. Prefers to be near freshwater lakes.

Food Insects caught on the wing. Mosquitoes make up a considerable portion of the diet.
Nest In woodpecker holes and natural tree cavities. At times in caves.

TREE SWALLOW *Tachycineta bicolor*

THE TREE SWALLOW RANGES throughout the majority of the United States, on through most of Canada and into Alaska. It is absent in the summer from the southern states and the plains areas of Oklahoma and Texas. In the winter, however, masses of these birds move into Florida, the Gulf Coast and southern Texas through to southern California.

This is a glossy blue/green swallow with slightly notched dark tail, the underparts are pure white and this white does not go above the eye, as seen in the violet-green swallow. Immature and first year birds are brown above and all white below.

This species is common in any open area from orchards, fields and salt marshes. Water is one of the principal requirements, and they also need dead snags for nesting sites. The birds do not excavate nesting holes but use ones created by woodpeckers in previous years. On occasion, a space under the eaves of a building will be chosen or even a cavity in a broken off portion of a tree. A good indication that it is a tree swallow nest is the presence of feathers. During the fall flocks of many thousands can often be seen lining power lines and covering buildings. They swirl in feeding masses over fields and upon finding berry-laden bushes will plunge down en masse to feed. These bushes appear to twinkle with the green/white bodies as they cling momentarily to grasp the fruit and then wing away.

The best way to encourage this species to visit your yard is to erect nesting boxes. An ideal box is 5 in square on the base and 6 in high. The $1^1/_2$ in opening should be centered 4 in above the floor. This is the typical swallow house but any variation may be occupied. They have even been known to occupy flicker houses! The box can be placed on a post out in the open. If placed on the side of a tree be sure it is facing a wide open, sunny area. The species competes with bluebirds for nesting boxes and other cavities so you have to make the choice of which species to attract during a nesting season.

FACTS AND FEATURES

5½ in

Plumage Glossy green to blue green above with line running below eye. Pure white below. Young birds brown backed. slight notch to tail.
Habitat Open areas near water; coastal areas. Prefers areas with dead trees.

Food Almost exclusively winged insects taken in flight. In fall, bayberries are taken in large quantities.
Nest In natural tree cavity, deserted woodpecker workings, nestboxes, eaves of buildings, cliff concavities.

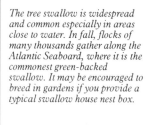

The tree swallow is widespread and common especially in areas close to water. In fall, flocks of many thousands gather along the Atlantic Seaboard, where it is the commonest green-backed swallow. It may be encouraged to breed in gardens if you provide a typical swallow house nest box.

♂

VIOLET-GREEN SWALLOW *Tachycineta thalassina*

THE VIOLET-GREEN SWALLOW RANGES from south Dakota and Nebraska, south through western Texas and on to the west coast. The summer range can extend north through eastern Canada and continues right into Alaska.

This common western swallow is very similar to the tree swallow with which it shares part of its range. It is brilliant green on the back and head and has pure white underparts. The white of the head extends above the eye and in the rump area there are significant white wraps up

This is the common swallow of the western states, where it may be found in a variety of habitats from woodland glades, canyons, mountainous areas and also within urban situations. It can be confused with the tree swallow, but you can distinguish it by its white flank patches, which almost meet above the tail.

♂

onto the sides. A further distinguishing mark is its short notched tail. Females are a brown color mixed with the green.

This is a bird of open areas, woodland glades and canyons. It can be found within the city and on the open strands of coastal beaches as well as in the mountains. This wide diversity of habitat makes it a commonly seen bird as a backyard visitor almost anywhere within its range.

Nest sites may be natural breaks in trees, abandoned nest holes of other species or crevices in rocky faces. With suitable conditions, groups of birds may nest in one area.

It is not as dependent on water as the tree swallow and this probably allows both to cohabitat one area. Masses of these birds can be seen "hawking" insects over open areas, on thermals rising in rocky sided canyons or skimming the sands of beaches.

The best way to lure these birds to your gardens or open areas is to erect suitable housing. As with the tree swallow a box with a 5 in square base with 6 in high walls and the $1\frac{1}{2}$ in opening centered 4 in above the floor is ideal. Place this on a post at a minimum of 5 ft off the ground.

Several of these nests can be placed out as these birds are gregarious when nesting. It is also interesting to watch helper birds raising young. These are birds that have not nested and are more than likely young from the recent year. They are termed "aunts" and they aid in bringing food to the young.

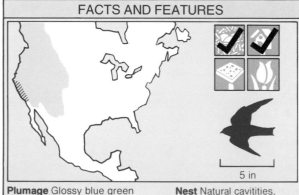

FACTS AND FEATURES

5 in

Plumage Glossy blue green back. White of underparts extending up rump and above the eye. Female clay brown.
Habitat Wide range from open forest and coastal bluffs to inner city locations.
Food Only insects caught on the wing have been reported in diet.

Nest Natural cavities, abandoned woodpecker holes, ledges in buildings, holes in cliff faces and nestboxes.

CLIFF SWALLOW *Hirundo pyrrhonota*

THE CLIFF SWALLOW RANGES THROUGHOUT the contiguous 48 states except for the area south of Virginia and east of Louisiana. It is found across the entire area of Canada and on into Alaska.

The orange buff rump, square tail and pale forehead coupled with the dark throat separate this species from all others seen in the United States. The cave swallow, which is confined to areas of Texas, is very similar but lacks the dark throat.

This is a swallow of open country in and around buildings. In some areas it reverts to the original nesting sites of cliffs or large rock faces. This is the swallow that has gained such notoriety at the Mission in San Juan Capistrano where each year they return to their nesting site on a given day in the spring. Indeed, throughout their range they are faithful to their nesting site each year unless disrupted or driven off.

The nest is a round structure with an elongated neck made of a myriad of mud balls. During the nesting season flocks can be seen at the edge of wet areas rolling up these mud balls, making endless trips to the nests which are placed up under the eaves or overhangs of buildings. The nest is lined with feathers upon completion. Gregarious nesters, they often cover whole walls with a hundred or so nests.

Though their range is extensive they do not nest densely throughout. In many instances your acquaintance will be with birds passing through your area, often in the company of other swallow species. These groups of birds will chase insects over meadows or swoop over water for food and drink. If, however, a suitable nesting site is nearby and a suitable surface for nesting is available, the creation of a wet area during nest building time can be an attraction for getting a colony started. A shallow pool in a muddy area can be created by simply allowing a spigot to drip constantly. The pooling area should be a fair size, large enough to allow several individuals to roll their mud balls at the same time. Feathers for lining the nest, scattered at the edges of these mud pools may be an attractant.

The cliff swallow builds a bulb-shaped nest, constructed from hundreds of mud balls which are cemented together and positioned under eaves, bridges or against sheltered cliffs. Its orange rump and square-ended tail distinguish it from all other species in this family, except for the very local cave swallow from which it differs in having a dark throat.

FACTS AND FEATURES

5½ in

Plumage Square tail and buffy orange rump and forehead. Orange cheeks, bluish back.
Habitat Open country in farmland and cliff areas; rural homes in canyons and along rivers.

Food Insects taken in air. In fall, "ballooning spiders" taken. A few berries may be consumed.
Nest Colonial nester. Builds gourd-shaped nest of rolled mud balls.

BARN SWALLOW *Hirundo rustica*

THIS SPECIES RANGES THROUGHOUT the lower 48 states except for Georgia, Florida and the Great Basin during the summer months. In the north its range runs through most of Canada and on into the panhandle of Alaska.

This is the best known of all the swallows as it has adapted to live directly with man. It is a metallic blue on the back with orange undersides and a rusty throat. The

The barn swallow is the only swallow with the combination of a deeply forked tail and rusty underparts. It may be encountered throughout much of North America where it is commonly found around farm buildings. Nests are made of an open cup of mud fixed to walls or rafters. May be seen in large flocks while preparing to migrate.

tail is deeply forked with two attenuated outer tail feathers.

The difference in the young birds is that they are very pale yellow on the forehead and throat and lack the extra long outer tail feathers.

This is the only passerine that is a cosmopolitan species. Its trim figure is an extremely common sight as its darts over fields and yards or along streams hunting for insects.

The grass and mud nest is placed in a wide variety of locations: on ledges inside farmbuildings, garages, or any building with open access. In addition road culverts, bridges, cliff faces and other natural sites are also chosen. The birds sitting on a power line or atop a tree twittering are the first indication that a site is being chosen. Then frequent trips of inspection are made before the nest is built. Once used the pair will remain faithful to the site as will their young, year after year. In migration they join with other swallows as they head south.

Because of their abundance and the way they investigate most buildings in the spring, they are likely to nest just about anywhere. The main requisite is that there should be an opening to the chosen site at all times. This does not have to be large. A missing pane of glass in a garage window is often enough as long as the nest can be placed up out of the way of constant activity. Nesting ledges can also be placed on sides of buildings. A 5 to 6 in square with a small lip running around it is ideal.

FACTS AND FEATURES

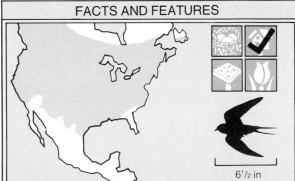

6½ in

Plumage Long, deeply forked tail; orange buff underparts; steel blue back; rusty throat. Female and young are duller.
Habitat Open areas, farmlands, waters edge. Canyons, desert regions and open mountain areas.
Food Mainly insects taken in flight. In fall, some berries are taken.

Nest A cup of mud pellets mixed with grasses and feathers. Placed on a ledge in building, on rock face, under bridges, culverts. Very rarely, in large hollow trees.

BLUE JAY *Cyanocitta cristata*

THE BLUE JAY RANGES FROM the eastern half of the United States from a line running roughly from the western edge of the Dakotas south to the east coast of Texas. Each year more and more birds are being seen west of this line. Summer range includes central and southeastern Canada.

Perhaps one of the best known of all birds the blue jay, with its bright blue coloration, is in every book we see as youngsters depicting a bird. It is all blue on the back with white in the wings, gray below and with a black necklace, and a distinctive crest to the head. Male and female are similar in pattern. A wide repetoire of calls is given, from the distinctive *jay-jay* that gives it its name, to imitations of red-shoulder hawks.

The species has fully adapted to living with people. It has a wide range of habitats from backyards to parks, farmland, woodlots, swamps and deep woods. It is certainly one of the boldest birds around. It constantly chases through the trees in small groups looking for other birds nests from which to plunder eggs, or it will actively chase cats, or scold and pester any hawk or owl it may encounter on these forays. In the yard, it is the dominant figure at the feeder and can "work out" how to get food from just about any type of feeder placed out.

There is no need to make an effort to attract this species! They will come to any type of feeder, and can often be seen hoarding the food they make off with in old bird nests, under shingles or under debris for future recovery. They will take every form of food from bread and cracked corn to peanut butter, suet, sunflower seeds

and the like. Often the nest is set up right in the area of the winter feeding station, a bulky mass of sticks in a tree crotch. If feeding continues through the summer the young will be brought to any feeder and supplied. They will also use bird baths on a daily basis. This has to be the easiest bird to attract with the least amount of effort. They also act as a warning system at the feeder should a cat or hawk attempt to take visiting birds.

FACTS AND FEATURES

11 in

Plumage Blue upperparts with white spotting in wings. Crest; black "necklace"; gray below; tail long and barred.
Habitat Forest and woodland areas; parks, orchards and gardens. Oak trees favored.

Food Acorns; beech nuts and others; tree mast. Insects, birds' eggs and nestlings, and even young mice and voles!
Nest A bulky, stick cup in oak, maple or beech (preferred) but also in conifers and large shrubs. Grapevine often used in buildings.

A well-known species of the eastern states, the blue jay is gradually spreading westwards. It prefers oak and pine woods, but has moved into many urban habitats where it has become remarkably tame. Easily attracted to the bird table for it will eat virtually anything that is offered. Unfortunately, it raids other birds' nests, taking both eggs and young.

BLACK-BILLED MAGPIE *Pica pica*

THE BLACK-BILLED MAGPIE ranges throughout the western United States from northern New Mexico and Arizona on through the plains of Nebraska and the Dakotas northwest through Canada and right into Alaska.

It is a very large, long-tailed bird, with a black back and hood, white underparts and green tail. In flight large white wing patches are visible.

In the Sacramento Valley of California you may be lucky to see the yellow-billed *(P Nuttalli)* species which occurs here.

A common inhabitant of open rangelands, open woodlands, thickets and city parks, they are highly gregarious and work areas in social groups. Being omniverous they can be seen feeding on a variety of food plants and foraging in areas from dump sites to cattle pens.

The nest is a very large bulky structure placed in a conifer or deciduous tree, and family units aid in raising the young. The loud *chak, chak, chak,* notes are a familiar sound in the west.

These birds are visitors to feeding stations where any type of food is taken. They require open areas, and will not come into feeders placed under trees or in a confined area. They are much more likely to investigate open lawn areas.

No matter how inventive you are, no man-made structure will entice this bird to nest, for it is a species that sets its own requirements and you will most often see it as it goes about its daily activites.

This is a very attractive, long-tailed, black and white crow with the blacks shot with purple and green. Distinguished in California from the yellow-billed magpie by its bill color. It has a liking for parklands, scrub and hedgerows, where it builds a large, domed nest. It is often found around feeding stations, but it will come to food only in open spaces.

FACTS AND FEATURES

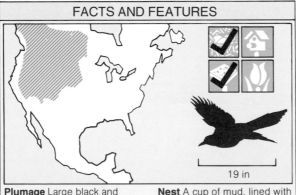

19 in

Plumage Large black and white bird with long metallic green tail. Large white wing patches in flight.
Habitat Open woodlands, conifer zones, rangelands and wooded foothills.
Food Animal and vegetable matter. Insects, seeds, berries, eggs, mice, carrion.

Nest A cup of mud, lined with rootlets, grass and hair inside a massive stick structure with side entrance.

AMERICAN CROW *Corvus brachyrhynchos*

This is the most widespread and abundant crow in North America — it is found in many different habitats except for the more arid zones. It often frequents rubbish tips and areas close to human habitation, where they become very tame. In some regions they are regarded as vermin, and because of this, are difficult to approach. It is a typical black corvid, which is best identified by its call in areas where the fish and northwestern crows occur.

THE AMERICAN CROW IS FOUND throughout the contiguous 48 states and in Canada. It is missing from western Texas and the Great Basin area, but will disperse into these areas in the winter.

This is perhaps one of the best known birds in the United States. Even the non-birdwatcher knows the crow. All black in color, it is similar in appearance to a few other corvids—the fish crow and the northwestern crow—and is best separated from them within overlap areas by its well known, distinctive *caw-caw-caw*.

This species has a widespread choice of habitat and can be found in parks or the deepest woodlands. It is especially responsive and adaptive to human occupation and disruption and takes quick advantage of food and nesting sites. Open dumping has done much to increase the numbers of this bird. During the nesting season they are a bit more reclusive. The bulky stick nest is placed in an assortment of sites depending on the region, from a crotch in an oak tree to a cliff ledge in a canyon. The young upon hatching follow the adults about, begging constant attention and food with raucous nasal calling. During the winter months, roosting congregations in the thousands are not uncommon.

In some areas they are considered to be vermin, and this has made the species wary of man. In most instances the presence of a human will set off the alarm of a watchful bird and off goes the flock. However, in some instances they will come into a backyard for corn, bread or other items they might be able to get at a feeder. Large trees in an area will encourage the birds to nest.

FACTS AND FEATURES

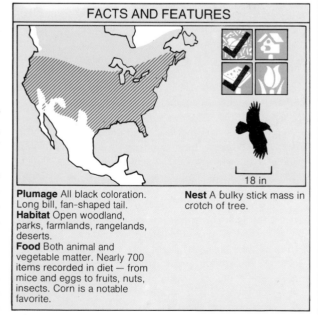

18 in

Plumage All black coloration. Long bill, fan-shaped tail.
Habitat Open woodland, parks, farmlands, rangelands, deserts.
Food Both animal and vegetable matter. Nearly 700 items recorded in diet — from mice and eggs to fruits, nuts, insects. Corn is a notable favorite.

Nest A bulky stick mass in crotch of tree.

CAROLINA CHICKADEE *Parus carolinensis*

Very similar to the black-capped chickadee, the Carolina chickadee has a neater black bib and secondaries, with no white edges. The black cap and bib, and white cheeks separate this from all other species over most of its range. The song usually comprises four notes, phee bee phee bay, while the chick-a-dee-dee *call is higher pitched and quicker than the black-capped.*

THIS IS THE SOUTHERN COUNTERPART of the black-capped chickadee and their ranges overlap to a slight extent in the Appalachians, Basically it is a resident from the northern border of New Jersey to central Florida and west to Oklahoma and the middle of the Texas coast. It does not tend to inhabit the elevations that the black-caps occupy in the Appalachians.

This is a difficult species to separate from the black-cap unless one considers the range. In basic appearance they are identical. This bird is slightly smaller, tends to have a more restricted bib marking and the sides look grayer due to the gray upper wing coverts. The song is a bit more musical and rapid than that of the black-cap but in areas of overlap the song patterns of the other species is quickly learned. Indeed in some regions hybridization has occurred.

As with its northern counterpart, the Carolina chickadee is found in a wide range of habitats from wooded swamplands, pinewoods, and open woodlots to gardens, parks and suburban backyards. Small bands occupy the same areas throughout life and usually represent a distinct family unit built up through the years. Within the group a specific song pattern is known and should other birds enter they are quickly detected. Trunks, limbs, and leaves are gleaned for insects, larvae and eggs. Berries and seeds are readily taken. The nest is in a hollow cavity either excavated by the birds or in an unused cavity originally used by other species.

This bird readily frequents the feeding tray and tends to be a visitor to backyards and gardens throughout the year. During the fall they often return with their young and introduce them to the feeding station. Oil-seed sunflower and sunflower are practically the exclusive seed taken at the station. Peanut butter with seeds in it and suet are also favorites. As with its northern counterpart, they accept nesting boxes readily.

FACTS AND FEATURES

Plumage Black cap, white cheek and black bib with distinct cut off to white of chest. Lacks white feather edging in wings.
Habitat Mixed woodlands, pine woods, gardens, parks, near habitation.
Food Mainly insectivorous. It also takes berries, seeds and other fruits.

Nest In natural cavity, abandoned nest hole or will excavate in soft wood.

4¹/₂ in

BLACK-CAPPED CHICKADEE *Parus atricapillus*

THIS SPECIES RANGES THROUGHOUT the northern portion of the United States, extending on up through Canada to Alaska. The southern limits of its range are northern California, northern New Mexico, the middle of Illinois and on through Pennsylvania and the southern border of New York. The population extends farther south only in the Appalachian mountains.

A small gray bird with a black cap and extensive black bib, its wings show marked gray on a dark background. The sides are a warm buff. Its call of *chick-a-dee-dee* is familiar in the north country. The drawn out mating call, a whistled *feee-beee* with a drop in pitch on the second phrase is often mistaken for a phoebe.

A resident of woodland, gardens, parkland, and city areas, it is one of the best known and trusting of the backyard visitors to the feeder. They come to a squeaking note produced by puckering the lips. Always investigating things and moving about, they very often stumble upon a predator such as a roosting owl. When this happens a milling group of scolding birds indicate that an unwanted predator is about.

The eggs are laid in a natural tree cavity, old woodpecker hole or an excavation made by the birds if the wood is soft enough. Food is a wide variety of items from berries and seeds to insect larvae and egg cases gleaned from limbs, trunks and undersides of leaves. In areas where outbreaks of pest species such as birch loopers or spruce bud worms occur, the chickadee populations greatly increase.

Certainly one of the commonest of feeding station birds throughout its range, at the feeding tray they favor sunflower seeds and oil-seed sunflower. They readily take peanut butter from holders and will feed heavily on suet during the winter months. Nesting can be encouraged by placing nest boxes on posts at the edge of woodlands or within an open wooded area. If placed in a too shaded area they usually will not be occupied. The nest box is best placed 5 to 10 ft off the ground. In size it is the standard for the group with a 4 in square base, and 8 in high sides. For successful nesting, there needs to be large trees in the area. If only new trees or young saplings are present, there are too few foraging areas to raise a family.

Over most of its range, the black cap and bib distinguish this chickadee. Where it overlaps the range of the Carolina chickadee, the white edges to the secondaries distinguish it, as do the phee bee phee bee song and the lower and slower call note. Where ranges overlap, this bird is usually found at higher elevations.

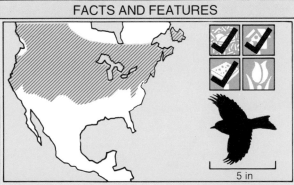

FACTS AND FEATURES

5 in

Plumage Black cap and bib. White cheeks and underparts. White edging to wing feathers.
Habitat Mixed forests, pine woods, swamplands, parks, orchards, backyards.
Food Mainly insects and invertebrates in summer. Winter diet of seeds and berries.

Nest Uses old woodpecker holes, natural cavitites or excavates own holes in soft wood.

TUFTED TITMOUSE *Parus bicolor*

THIS SPECIES RANGES THROUGH the eastern half of the United States from western Texas to southern Minnesota east to the coast. They do not live in the extreme southern tip of Florida.

The tufted titmouse is a gray bird with a head crest, dark button eyes and orange tinted sides. Throughout most of the range the head crest is gray but in southern Texas the crest is black. The call is a resounding *peter, peter, peter* that seems much too loud for a bird this size.

An inquisitive species, it usually roams the woodlands with its near relative the chickadee. A wide variety of habitat is frequented from parkland, orchards, mesquite areas to backyards in cities. These birds are hole nesters and will use old nest sites of woodpeckers, natural cavities in trees or birdboxes. When soft wood is encountered they can excavate their own site.

This is a classic bird feeder visitor. Relatively tame they come readily to the feeding station. Peanut hearts, peanut butter with seeds, suet cakes, sunflower seeds etc., are all favorite foods. Visitation to feeders will be almost like clockwork and very often they will sit close by as the feeders are filled. Be sure to provide ample cover nearby should a predator attempt an attack. Nesting boxes can be placed out at the edges of wooded areas on posts or affixed to a tree. These should be 4 in square at the base by 8 in high; the $1\frac{1}{4}$ in hole centered 6 in above the floor. The box can be as low as 4 ft off the ground and should not exceed 10 ft for best results.

Once the feeding station has been accepted these birds will be year-round residents of the area and will often bring their young to the sites in the fall. In the spring they will start their "mutual feeding" prior to nesting.

FACTS AND FEATURES

Plumage Gray bird with crest. Black crest in Texas form. Orange sides, whitish underparts.
Habitat Deciduous woodlands, swamplands, coniferous forest, orchards, parks, backyards.
Food Seventy percent of the diet is insect matter. Also seeds and berries.

Nest In a cavity: natural, or one abandoned by woodpeckers or excavated in soft wood. Lined with leaves.

6 in

The large size, gray crest, blackish forehead and lack of black bib distinguish this bird. Small flocks are often found outside the breeding season, and stream edges are a favored feeding area in woodland.

BUSHTIT *Psaltriparus minimus*

THE BUSHTIT IS A PERMANENT RESIDENT from western coastal Washington and eastern Oregon through Utah and Wyoming and south into western Texas. An isolated population occurs on the Edwards Plateau of Texas.

Twittering little bands of this diminutive bird seem suddenly to appear in shrubs and bushes. They are dark gray above and a lighter gray below, and the flanks may have a pink tint to them. In one form in the extreme southwest, a black mask is present. The tail is quite long for such a small bird.

Most of the year these birds travel about in social groups of up to 20 birds. They seem to "stream" from one shrub to another and actively forage about on the outer limbs like mice. They also hang upside down to secure food and glean the insects, egg cases and larvae that make up the majority of their diet from beneath twigs and leaves. Usually a constant low *twittering* can be heard that keeps the flock in contact with one another. During the breeding season they break up into pairs and a rather elaborate, well made pendulant nest is placed low down in a small tree or dense shrub. The preferred habitat is oak/juniper woodlands and sidehills along with the unique vegetation known as chaparral on the west coast.

They frequent parks, inner city gardens and often wander about wherever there are trees. It is not the type of bird you can attract with a feeding station or nest box. However, they will forage in well planted situations seeking out the insects that are attracted to garden areas. If brush piles are provided and there is an adequate food supply, nesting could occur.

FACTS AND FEATURES

4¹/₂ in

Plumage Very small, long tailed gray bird. Can have black mask, dark line or brownish area near eye depending on race.
Habitat Mixed woodlands, chaparral, pinyon-juniper woodlands, scrub, oak.
Food Eighty-five percent insect matter; some seeds and berries.

Nest Large, pendant mass of twigs, grasses, moss and lichens bound by plant fiber and spider web. Side entrance near top. In tree or dense bushes.

The long tail, drab appearance and short bill help to identify this bushtit. On the west coast, the birds have a brown crown. Inland birds have brown ear coverts and the southwestern birds favor high elevations and have a black mask.

RED-BREASTED NUTHATCH *Sitta canadensis*

THE RED-BREASTED NUTHATCH is very widespread throughout the northern portion of North America on into Alaska, down the western mountains into Arizona and in the east through New England and down the Appalachians. In winter, the birds are seen throughout the remainder of the United States, except for the extreme southern portion of Florida and Texas.

The male is a small, active bird with a black cap, distinct white eye line and a black line through the eye, a gray back and rusty underparts. The throat area is white. The female is a much paler version. As with all nuthatches, they move headfirst down trees.

They tend to be a bird of the coniferous areas, though in migration may appear in any type of vegetation. More of a gleaner of the outer branches and twigs of the trees than its white-breasted "cousin," the two live in the same areas of overlapping range. The call is a very rapid high pitched and nasal *teent, teent, teent* likened by some to the sound of a tin horn. The nest is in an abandoned hole, natural cavity or softwood excavation made by the birds themselves. An identification method for this species is the ring of pine, fir or balsam resin that is smeared around the entrance.

This is an irruptive migrant species. In some years incredible numbers migrate, and during these times remnant populations frequently stay behind and nest in "out of normal range" areas. These movements are based on the state of the conifer seed crop of the north.

They come to feeder sites, where sunflower seeds are preferred. Suet is also taken readily as is peanut butter and seeds. Usually the food is taken elsewhere and cracked open or stored for future consumption. As with the white-breasted nuthatch, nesting boxes will be occupied. The construction is the same as listed under that species, however, pine bark will greatly enhance the possibility of occupation. When pine resin appears at the entrance area, you will know that the nuthatches have accepted it.

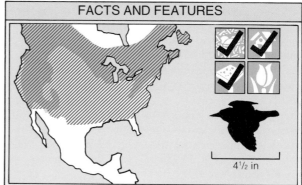

FACTS AND FEATURES

4½ in

Plumage Small, gray back; black cap; white eye line and black line through eye. Buffy to rusty underparts.
Habitat Mainly coniferous woodlands but into mixed woodlands especially during irruption years.
Food Insects, egg cases, pine seeds, mixed berries and fruit.

Nest Excavates hole in dead stump of soft wood or takes over abandoned woodpecker hole. Usually adds resin around entrance.

The black crown, white supercilium and black line through the eye are the best identification features. Males have bright rusty underparts, and females are duller about the head and on the underparts.

WHITE-BREASTED NUTHATCH *Sitta carolinensis*

THIS SPECIES RANGES THROUGHOUT the United States but is absent from the central belt from mid-Wyoming to Texas and from some western mountain areas.

The male has a black cap (gray in the female) which contrasts sharply with the all white underparts and face area. The back is a dark gray. The flank area is a rusty color, and more pronounced in western subspecies. The nuthatches are the only birds that consistently travel headfirst down a tree. This allows them the opportunity to discover food items missed by the other species which forage from the base upward.

This bird is well known throughout the country, and the call, a rapid nasal *yank, yank, yank* is a familiar sound of woodlands. In the east it is found in deep woodlands, swampy areas, orchards, parks and indeed any locality with large trees. In the west, oak and coniferous woodlands are preferred. The nest is placed in a natural cavity, abandoned woodpecker hole or a site excavated by the birds themselves if the wood is not too hard.

Having adapted well to life within suburban and city areas, the nuthatch often shows up in yards or gardens. They come readily to feeding stations and take mainly sunflower seeds. They fly off with the seeds, wedge them into a bark crevice or under a house shingle and pound away with their sharp bills. They will often hoard seeds in old abandoned bird nests or tree crevices. Suet is also taken particularly in the winter. They will accept nesting boxes with a 4 in square base and 10 in high sides. This deep nest duplicates the nesting holes they normally use. The entrance hole should be placed near the top and be 1¼ inches in diameter. In addition, it has been shown that they prefer the box to be covered with bark sections. The nest can be fixed to the trunk or large limb of a tree at the edge of a woodland, or actually in the woodland, and should be about 12 ft off the ground.

The larger size, white face and breast distinguish this nuthatch from red-breasted. The rusty color of the rear underparts is variable. The song consists of several low, nasal whistling notes.

FACTS AND FEATURES

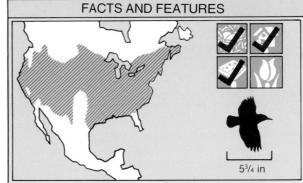

5¾ in

Plumage Blue gray back; black cap (in male, gray in female); white underparts with rust flanks. Thin bill.
Habitat Deciduous, mixed and coniferous forests, parklands.
Food Insects and spiders, seeds, nuts and berries.

Nest In a natural cavity or one abandoned by a woodpecker. Or excavated by birds in soft wood.

♀

♂

BROWN CREEPER *Certhia americana*

The streaky brown plumage and white underparts distinguish this bird. It moves in short jerks spiraling up the tree trunk, with its long, stiff tail feathers acting as a prop.

IN THE WEST the range of the brown creeper extends from southern Alaska through the western mountains to extreme western Texas. In the eastern portion of North America breeding occurs in the Great Lakes region east through New England and south in the Appalachian mountains.

This small, sleek bird is often to be seen creeping its way up tree trunks in search of food. Mottled brown on the back with a tawny rump, it has white underparts and a white line over the eye. The dark bill is long and curved. The long tail has stiff feather tips to support the bird while climbing. In flight a buffy wing patch is obvious.

This species is rather inconspicuous in the woodlands as it makes its way up a tree trunk in a spiral, searching for insects' egg cases, larvae or adults. Its movements are jerky as it inspects each crevice then hops up to another spot using its tail as a prop. The song is a musical trill and is accompanied by darting flights in and around tree trunks.

The nest is placed in a most unusual spot. The birds find loosened bark, often in a swampy area, and wedge the nest between the bark and the tree trunk. To get to the nest the birds slip behind the bark and "disappear" from sight.

Large trees in the vicinity are essential to attract these birds all year round. However, during migration, when many are moving south, they often show up in the most bizarre places—on the side of buildings, telephone poles and the like.

Though almost totally dependent on insect materials, in the winter they will come to suet feeders. Seeds are not taken but on occasion birds will make regular visits to feeders with peanut butter. Their unique nesting habits negate the use of nesting boxes but clusters of up to 10 birds have been found spending cold winter nights huddled in the floor of bluebird boxes at woodland edges.

FACTS AND FEATURES

5 in

Plumage Streaked brown plumage; white eye line; curved bill. Rusty rump; pointed tail feathers; white underparts.
Habitat Mixed woodlands, coniferous wood, swamps. In migration; anywhere.

Food Insects: larvae, pupae, adults in bark crevices. Also spiders. A few seeds may be taken.
Nest Difficult to locate. Wedged under loose bark. , Made of twigs, bark strips and feathers.

CAROLINA WREN *Thryothorus ludovicianus*

This is the largest wren of the north east, and you can identify it by its rusty upperparts, white eye stripe and throat, and its warm buffy underparts. It is often found near streams in its favored habitat of thick underbrush in open woodland

THIS SPECIES IS FOUND from southern New England, west to south Iowa then south through mid-Texas. Range is affected by harshness of winter. Mild winters see northward extensions while severe winters force the population south and kill many birds.

A rusty brown bird with rich buff yellow underparts, the Carolina wren has a white throat and a distinct white line over the eye. A very active bird, it is also a constant singer. Perched in an opening in the underbrush with head thrown back its loud, ringing *chewee, cheweee, chewee* call, in places interpreted as *tea-kettle, tea-kettle, tea-kettle* is an unforgettable song. The song can be heard on any warm day at any time of year.

A skulker in the dense underbrush and thicket, it will make forays out into the open to sing, or when attracted to scolding sounds. You can often see it hunched over, peering out of the thicket at you. A wide range of habitat is chosen as long as it has dense undercover—swamplands, parks, brush lots, woodlots and backyards. The nest in swamps and woodlands is placed in any open niche from tree stump to leaf-covered hillside. In the vicinity of houses any opening may be chosen, including tops of fuel tanks, in old discarded teapots and even in the pockets of pants hung in garages.

Foraging for food in the winter months, this species is not dependent on feeders. However, water in a birdbath is welcome. In the winter when they do come to the feeding station, suet and peanut butter are both taken. Some seeds are taken but on a very limited basis. Oil-seed sunflower is the favorite.

One of the best attractants is a large, dense brush pile. If the birds are in the area they are sure to find it. Nesting boxes may be used if placed on a pole near the brush pile or dense underbrush. A box 4 in square at the base and 8 in high with an $1^1/_2$ in diameter hole is ideal. This may be used as a roost site also.

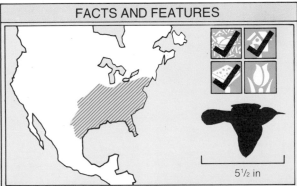

FACTS AND FEATURES

5½ in

Plumage Rich chestnut brown upperparts; bright white eye line; buffy yellow below. Long tail and long curved bill.
Habitat Shrubby areas and thicket of gardens, parkland, forest edges. Loves brush piles. In and around buildings.

Food Insects and all types of invertebrates. In winter takes seeds.
Nest Bulky mass of twigs, grasses and leaves that may be placed in any dark cavity. From tree stump to jacket pocket on clothes line!

HOUSE WREN *Troglodytes aedon*

THIS SPECIES RANGES THROUGHOUT most of the United States except south of a belt running from the Texas panhandle to southern Georgia. In the winter they migrate into this range, and on into Mexico. Summer range includes central and southern parts of Canada.

A rather plain brown bird, it is lacking any distictive field marks outside of some flank barring and a hint of an eye line. The tail is rather long and carried cocked at an angle. Several races occur across North America. The song is loud and bubbling.

A bird of brushy areas, it is fond of dense shrub and brush pile. It frequents parks, orchards, woodlots and gardens. Deep woodland is not this bird's area. It has adapted well to living within cities and suburbs and takes readily to nesting boxes. In natural nesting, the nest is placed in any available concavity—old woodpecker holes, broken off limbs, brush tangles. Often such cavities are filled to the brim with material. A builder of dummy nests, any concavity in the area will be filled with material purportedly acting as a confusion element to predators and to cut down on site availability for other competitive pairs.

Being exclusive insect eaters, they are most often gone before an active feeding station is in gear. In areas where they occur in the winter, suet and peanut butter will be taken. They will readily take to a nesting box placed out. In fact they often fill every nesting box within the vicinity. The box should be about 4 in square at the base and 8 in high. A 1 in diameter hole should be centered 6 in above the floor. The box can be placed on a post or tree that is in the open or at a field edge. Of all the nesting box species, this bird is the easiest to attract. Once in, singing will come from all parts of the yard and the bird will be seen busily searching for food in every possible place.

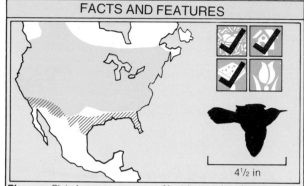

FACTS AND FEATURES

Plumage Plain brown coloration lacking any distinct marks. Buff eye line; long tail.
Habitat Open woodlands, scrubby hillsides, thick understory. Parks, gardens, backyards.
Food All animal matter in diet. Insects, spiders, larval forms.

Nest In a cavity of tree or stub or in birdhouse. Bulky mass of sticks. Will dummy nest and fill all birdhouses in territory with mock nests!

4½ in

Although characteristic of orchards and farmyards, this wren (above) has adapted well to living within urban areas, for it will readily use nest boxes. More normal breeding sites include natural cavities in trees and old woodpecker holes (left).

Best distinguished from other wrens by the lack of any obvious head markings. The almost plain underparts, longer tail and larger size distinguish it from the winter wren. It is very energetic and has the habit of cocking its tail over its back. A summer visitor, it winters in the Atlantic and Gulf States.

WINTER WREN *Troglodytes troglodytes*

Generally very retiring, this wren may be attracted to gardens by brush piles. In spring, the song is enthusiastically given from an open perch. It lasts for about five seconds and consists of a rapid succession of high notes and trills.

IN THE WEST the winter wren occupies a thin coastal band from Alaska to southern California. It crosses central Canada and inhabits the Great Lakes region on the east through New England and down the Appalachians.

A tiny, active species, it is a rich chestnut in color, with paler chin and underbelly. The flanks are conspicuously striped. The very short, rusty tail is carried cocked at a high angle. The explosive *je-jit* note is often an indication that it is skulking in a thicket on its winter range. Within the breeding areas the loud, bubbling, very musical call flows on and on in ecstatic exuberance.

A secretive skulker of woodland streams, deep wood areas and mountain forests, for nesting it seems to prefer areas with a stream nearby, the tinkling song contrasting with the bubbling sounds of the current. The domed nest of plant materials and mosses is lined with feathers. It may be placed in a natural cavity, old woodpecker hole, rock crevice or on the ground at the base of a tree. The male is polygamous and therefore there are usually several nests in the area occupied at one time. In such instances the mating occurs at set intervals allowing the male to help with raising the young in hatching succession. During the winter they move south as far as Florida and the Gulf Coast.

Due to their secretive nature and preference for deep woodland nesting, nest boxes do not attract this species. However, during cold winter nights boxes have been used as roost sites. They rely mainly on insect matter and some wild seeds and rarely come to a feeder. When they do, suet seems to be the only attractant. However, they will use brush piles. A large brush pile that has been untouched for some time will not only provide cover but will be an area rich with food material. Such a pile may see a bird in residence through the winter. The pile should be placed in dense cover. This species will not frequent the open.

FACTS AND FEATURES

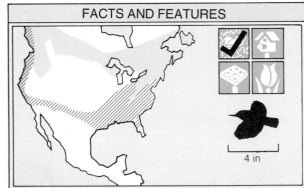

4 in

Plumage Dark brown; very short tail; eye line; heavily barred flanks.
Habitat Dense coniferous forest, deep woodland, ravines, thicketed areas, brushy piles, parks and gardens.
Food All sorts of invertebrates. Insects: adults, eggs and larvae; also spiders.

Nest A ball shaped structure with side entrance. Moss and twigs, lined with feathers. Placed in crevice or depression on or near ground.

96

RUBY-CROWNED KINGLET *Regulus calendula*

THE RUBY–CROWNED KINGLET ranges in the east, only in northern New England in the summer, but from New Jersey south through Florida and the Gulf States in the winter. In the west, the summer population is found from Oregon and middle Montana, south mid-California, south Arizona and New Mexico. Winter populations build up in this area, and cover the more southern sections. Summer range includes most of Canada and Alaska.

A very small, greenish gray bird, it has distinct wing bars and a broken eye ring. Underparts may take on a yellowish tint. The male has brilliant red crown feathers that are usually covered by other head feathers. In display or when agitated, the crown feathers are held erect. Constantly on the move, a persistent flicking of the wings is a good field mark. The song is a loud outburst of clear introductory notes and rolling bubbling.

This species is common in thicketed areas and woodlands with good undergrowth during migration and on wintering grounds. During the breeding season coniferous woodlands are its home. The nest is a cup made of plant fibers, grasses and shredded bark. If *Usnea* lichen is available it will be incorporated into the nest. The nest tends to be a pendulous structure but at times is positioned directly on a branch or at the very tops of spruce or other conifers.

Visiting woodlands and dense underbrush is the best way to become acquainted with this species. No specific plantings will attract them. Birds that opt to spend the winter in the northern part of the United States will at times come to a feeder and can be seen hovering at the suet bag picking off small bits. An oil-seed will be taken and hammered at, much in the same fashion as a chickadee opening a seed.

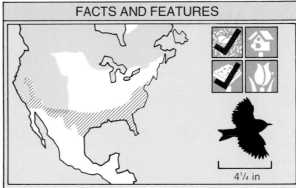

FACTS AND FEATURES

4¼ in

Plumage Tiny; active; grayish olive to yellowish green. Eye ring and wing bars. Male has brilliant ruby crown, most often concealed in head feathers.
Habitat Prefers coniferous woodlands during breeding season, otherwise mixed woodlands, thickets.

Food Insects, spiders, egg cases. Some fruit in winter.
Nest Tight cup of mosses, lichens and plant down. In a conifer, in most cases often quite low to ground.

This bird can be mistaken for a warbler during the fall, but it is much smaller, shorter-tailed, and its habit of flicking its wings is a very good field characteristic. It prefers conifer woods, where it may be seen to hover before shoots in order to pick off insects.

♀

♂

GOLDEN-CROWNED KINGLET *Regulus satrapa*

THE SUMMER RANGE OF THIS BIRD includes the mountain areas of the east and west. During the winter it is found throughout the contiguous 48 states and in southern central Canada.

This tiny bird is usually first detected by its high pitched tsee-tsee-tsee notes that are just within the upper limits of hearing. An olive-backed bird, with gray underparts and double wing bars, it has a white line running through the eye and an orange crown bordered with yellow is seen in the male. The female lacks the orange crown but has a rich yellow color in that area. Constantly on the move, its wings have a "nervous twitch."

A bird of the coniferous woods, it spreads on into deciduous forest during migration and wintering periods. Usually it will remain in the upper crowns of the trees. It attracts readily if a squeaking imitation is made to resemble the scold of another bird. The nest is a small cup of plant fibers, lined with grasses and placed high in a conifer, usually out near the branch tip, making it a very inaccessible nest to get to for a predator such as a red squirrel. It appears to have a cyclic pattern that follows the build up of insect species such as the spruce bud worms. Following such summers the birds appear in great numbers on their wintering grounds.

Conifers are sure to attract this species—in general they prefer larger, densely packed trees. Spruce is the favorite among the conifers. Though they do not usually come to feeding trays, they will often come to a suet feeder during periods of very severe winter weather.

Another attractant is peanut butter with seeds. This can be mixed up and placed in cups nailed to a board and fastened to a tree, or in cavities drilled out in limbs, boards or logs fixed to a feeding tray. As with most birds, open water will also attract them in winter.

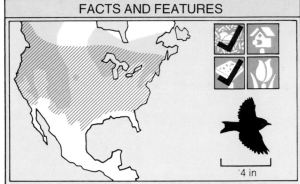

FACTS AND FEATURES

Plumage Olive green above; white eye line with black line through eye; bright yellow crown. Red center to crown in male. Light underparts.
Habitat Mainly coniferous woods during breeding season. Mixed forest during the rest of the year.

Food Insects in all forms, from eggs to pupae and larvae. Spiders and some berries in winter.
Nest A deep cup of plant down, mosses and lichens placed in a conifer and very often near the top.

This bird is common in coniferous woodlands, but spreads into deciduous forests in winter months. A very small warbler-like species which cannot be mistaken because of its head stripes. The call is a very high pitched see which is only just audible.

BLUE-GRAY GNATCATCHER *Polioptila caerulea*

In recent years, the range of this bird increased dramatically toward the north. It is a species of the tree tops where is flycatches for food. The habit of moving its long tail sideways is characteristic. It is sometimes referred to as the miniature mockingbird.

THIS SPECIES HAS EXTENDED its range northward dramatically in the last 20 years. Found from New Hampshire and Vermont south through Florida and west to California, it is absent from the northern great plains area and northwest America.

An active, long tailed bird that is steel blue gray above, it has a black tail that has white outer feathers, is mainly white below and has a distinct white eye ring. The cap may appear darker, especially in the male. The action of hopping along a branch with tail swinging from side to side is distinctive. The thin, high pitched *tseeee* is usually the first giveaway that the bird is feeding up in the canopy. The song is a rather loud rollicking whistling song alternating with wheezing notes. It is known by some as the "miniature mockingbird."

This species frequents woodlands, swamps, thickets and coastal chaparral. Very active and not really secretive, they usually attract readily to "squeaking." The nest is a beautiful structure of woven plant down and fibers bound by cobwebs and then covered with lichen flakes. It is usually placed well up in a tree and often near water. The two adults are bundles of activity when caring for the tiny young.

Mainly encountered as it passes through the garden in migration, if large trees and water are available it may nest. Insects attracted to nearby plantings might attract the adults especially while they are concerned about raising their young.

FACTS AND FEATURES

4½ in

Plumage Blue gray above and white below. Long tail with white outer tail feathers.
Habitat Mixed forests, oak woods, chaparral, pinyon pine groves, dense hillside thickets.
Food Mainly insects and variety of other invertebrates including spiders.

Nest A beautiful small cup of plant down and covered with spider web and lichens. Straddles limb and has the appearance of a bump on the limb.

EASTERN BLUEBIRD *Sialia sialis*

The throat, sides of neck and flanks are chestnut, contrasting with the white belly and bright blue upperparts of this bird. The female is duller, but with a clear, whitish eye ring. The pleasant warbling song is a series of chur-lee chur-lee notes.

THIS SPECIES RANGES THROUGH the eastern half of North America from southeast Canada south through mid-Texas. They are permanent within that range from Connecticut and central New York.

The male has deep blue upperparts contrasting with a rich reddish rust below, with white underbelly. The female is a pale version of the male. Young birds are very heavily spotted as with all the thrushes.

Bluebirds are among the best known of the songbirds. Their beautiful colors coupled with a soft, musical warbling excite people no matter how often seen or heard. Their flight is bouyant as they drop from atop a small tree to gather up an insect and return to the tree perch. Favored habitat is woodland edge, farmfields and orchards. Loss of such habitat in the east, in particular, has affected population. In addition, being a hole-nesting species, competition with starlings, and in some areas house sparrows, has placed an additional stress on populations. Favored nesting areas are holes in dead snags at field edges. To arrest the decline a massive bluebird nesting box project has been undertaken with dramatic results in many areas.

Though not a visitor to feeding stations, they may come to gardens for food and certainly will inhabit fields, pastures and orchards if available. To encourage nesting, a specific bluebird nesting box can be constructed. The floor should be 5 in square, and the sides 10 in at the back sloping to 9 in in front. The hole must be $1^1/2$ in in diameter and placed just over 1 in from the top of the front panel. A collar-like flange should be placed around the hole so that it extends $1^1/2$ in out. It acts as an anti-

blue jay barrier to prevent the birds from reaching the bottom if they try to steal eggs. This box should be placed on a post 3 to 5 ft above the ground and a minimum of 25 ft from the nearest tree, well out in the open. A site in an orchard or field is perfect. You must actively monitor box use and discard any attempts at building by house sparrows. Once the young bluebirds have fledged, discard the material in the box and clean it out. Bluebird trails have been very successful.

FACTS AND FEATURES

7 in

Plumage Striking blue above; red chestnut throat, neck and upper breast. White lower belly. Female much duller.
Habitat Open woodland edges, farmlands, garden, orchards.
Food Seventy-five percent of diet is insect material; the rest is berries other fruits and seeds.

Nest A cup of twigs placed in a natural cavity, abandonded nest hole or nest box.

WESTERN BLUEBIRD *Sialia mexicana*

THIS BIRD IS RESIDENT in a narrow coastal strip from Washington to southern California crossing through Nevada and south through Arizona and New Mexico. Summer populations extend east into extreme western Montana and project north from New Mexico into Colorado and Utah.

This species is a deeper blue than the eastern bluebird and has a blue throat. The chestnut red of the upper belly extends over onto the back while the lower belly is white. The female has a grayish head, powder blue wings and a red tinted breast.

The western bluebird frequents woodland glades, orchards, meadows, farmlands and, in the winter, the mesquite areas of deserts. The plight of this western bird has not been as dramatic as the eastern species due to the fact that the habitat has remained more stable. In addition, the starling and house sparrow do not frequent much of the habitat this species occupies.

The nest is in a hole of a tree or fence post, and open pine woods are a particularly favored spot in mountainous areas. Upon fledging, the male raises the young while the female re-nests.

Not really a feeder bird, the areas they frequent for the most part have adequate year-round food supplies. Populations that move into desert regions enjoy feeding on mistletoe and other berry types as an alternative to insects. They will nest in bluebird boxes and do not seem to be as fussy as the eastern birds. A box with a 5 in base,

8 in in height with a 1¹/₂ in diameter hole placed near the top is perfect. This can be placed on a post 5 to 10 ft off the ground or fixed to a tree at a woodland edge. Though they like open areas, they do not need the large expanse of space required around a nesting box that the eastern bluebird requires.

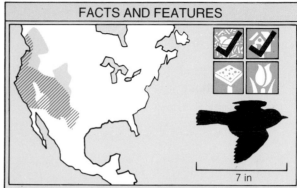

FACTS AND FEATURES

7 in

Plumage Upperparts a deep bluish purple. Chestnut red on breast and back; throat blue; underbelly white.
Habitat Open coniferous woods, mixed forest clearings, farmlands, orchards, deserts. In winter mesquite mistletoe groves in west.

Food Mainly insects, spiders and other invertebrates. Berries in winter.
Nest In a tree cavity, abandoned hole or nesting box.

The deeper blue in the upperparts and on the throat distinguish this bird from the eastern bluebird. The belly and undertail coverts are also gray, and not white. Some chestnut shows on the shoulders of the male. Females are duller and have a gray throat. The call is a phew *and the song is a continuation of this note,* phew-phew phewee.

♂

♀

VEERY *Catharus fuscescens*

The male and female veery are similar. The song, a siren of descending notes veer, veer, veer, *is very distinctive and the call is a low* phew. *Its spotted breast, gray flanks, lack of eye ring and tawny upperparts distinguish it.*

THE VEERY IS A SUMMER RESIDENT in a thin band across the northern section of the country. Found throughout New England in the Great Lakes region and on the west through Canada, there is a population pocket in Montana, Idaho, Wyoming, northern Utah and Colorado in the mountains.

There are several subspecific forms of this species— the back color of eastern birds is a light rust whereas the western forms have almost brown backs. There is no distinct eye ring, and the spotting on the throat and extreme upper breast is very pale in the eastern form, and more bold in the western. The sides are a dusted gray.

A bird of the dense forest, stream sides and mixed deciduous coniferous woods, in the east it favors hemlock groves. A good deal of its time is spent running about in short bursts, pausing to look for food and running on. It is a very tame and confiding species and will often approach to within a few feet if you stand still. Along river and stream edges they can often be seen foraging among the rocks and on mossy banks for insects.

The nest is almost always on the ground tucked into a depression among the leaves, and covered by the lush vegetation of the moist area chosen. The eggs are a dazzling blue when seen in the low light of these secluded spots.

A wet area is needed with mixed conifer and broad-leaved trees to attract this species. If such a location is available, the haunting down-spiraling flute-like notes will indicate that the veery has taken up residence. During migration they may also appear in garden areas especially if a sheltered, moist area such as a fern garden is provided.

FACTS AND FEATURES

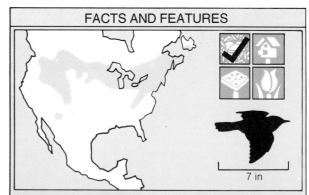

Plumage Uniform reddish brown to brown above. Very diffuse spotting on buff throat; white underbelly.
Habitat Moist woodlands, conifers, swamplands, thickets at river edge.
Food Insects, spiders and other invertebrates. Has been seen to take land snails and berries in fall.

Nest Built on or close to ground. Cup of grasses and leaves, lined with rootlets.

7 in

HERMIT THRUSH *Catharus guttatus*

THIS SPECIES RANGES IN THE EAST throughout New England, over into the Great Lakes region, all across Canada and on into Alaska where it can be found nearly to the Kotzebue peninsula. In the west, there is a resident population in the extreme coastal strip from Washington to California. In summer the birds are found through the mountainous sections from Montana to Arizona. In the southern part of the United States this is the winter thrush, wintering from southern New England through to Florida and west through Texas.

This is a highly variable looking species, depending on where you see it within its range. For example, interior Alaska has a diminutive form almost an inch shorter than the eastern subspecies. In coloration the back ranges from a rich brown to olive brown to pale washed-out light brown. In each case, however, the tail tends to be a contrasting rust color and is often pumped up and down after the bird moves across the ground or sits up on a limb. The underparts are white with concentrated spotting on the throat tapering off on the sides.

Known as the "swamp angel," because of its beautiful song, it is considered by many the finest songster in North America. The flute-like quality with ringing two-toned notes is memorable when echoing from a deep coniferous forest glade. Favored habitats are dense conifer forests, woodland thickets in swamp areas and mixed forest sidehills in the mountains. A fairly shy species, it tends to keep a lot of vegetation between it and the viewer. A lot of time is spent on, or close to, the ground as it forages about with short hops and runs, then long pauses looking for prey. Berries are taken in winter in the north.

This species is mainly seen as a migrant unless the area has extensive deep woodlands or coniferous forests. Wintering birds are reluctant to come near feeders but on occasion have to come to suet. Privet, bittersweet, and honeysuckle berries can be planted for winter feeding.

FACTS AND FEATURES

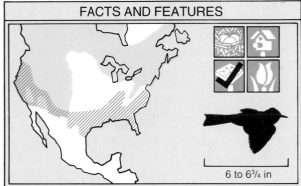

6 to 6¾ in

Plumage Olive brown to gray brown upperparts and chestnut rusty tail. Buffy flanks. Spotting of upper breast triangular in shape.
Habitat Coniferous woodlands, mixed wooded areas and swamps
Food Insects, spiders, small snails, berries and seeds.

Nest Compact cup of twigs, grass and rootlets. Outside usually made of ferns and mosses.

The reddish tail in all forms of this bird help to distinguish it from similar thrushes. It often flicks its wings when raising its tail. The call note is a soft chuck, and dead trees are a favorite song perch.

WOOD THRUSH *Hylocichla mustelina*

THIS SPECIES RANGES FROM the eastern half of the United States from the western Minnesota border south through mid-Nebraska and the eastern half of Texas. The southern terminus on the east coast is extreme northern Florida.

An alert thrush of the lower undergrowth in forests, it is bright reddish brown above with rich color on the head and nape of the neck. The eye ring blends with the light streaked ear region. Underparts are white with large distinct spots running from the throat to the underbelly. The legs are a rich orange.

A common bird of the swamps and woodlands, it stays mainly in the undergrowth of the forest and on the ground, and relishes the cool shadows of the forest. The rich, flute-like music is duet-like in quality with its pure whistles and extended trills. The call note is a distinctive *pit-pit-pit*. Usually the nest is placed in the crotch of a sapling or scrub tree about 10 ft off the ground. It is a cup of grasses and leaves with a middle layer of mud. The mud within the nest is typical of all the thrushes. Upon hatching, the two adults usually separate with the brood, each taking two and raising them.

Dense undergrowth is a prerequisite for this species. In an area where saplings are always present the chance of this species nesting increases. Once a forest reaches maturity so the canopy development negates undergrowth, the birds may use it for migration or feeding purposes but it will not be suitable for nesting. Water is another attractant and a stream or brooklet running through an area is definitely a plus. They do not come to feeding stations and the majority of the population leave the United States completely in winter.

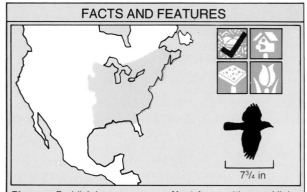

FACTS AND FEATURES

Plumage Reddish brown above with bright rusty tint to nape and crown. Underparts white with distinct spotting.
Habitat Prefers cool, understory near brooklets. Swamps, understory of mixed woods.
Food Insects, worms, invertebrates, larvae, berries, seeds.

Nest A cup with a mud lining covered with grasses. The outside is made of grass, plant stems, leaves and grapevine.

7³/₄ in

The wood thrush is the commonest nesting thrush to be found in eastern, deciduous woods and suburban gardens, where it prefers the forest understory. It is distinguished from thrashers by its shorter tail, dark eyes and spotted breasts.

ROBIN *Turdus migratorius*

A familiar species which is often encountered on lawns in city parks and gardens searching for insects and earthworms. In winter, it will eat berries and may be attracted to gardens by fruit-bearing trees. Juveniles have spotted breasts.

ONE OF THE MOST WIDESPREAD of all bird species in North America, the robin is found throughout the United States and Canada. During the winter months the majority of the population moves south but tends to stay year-round in most of the contiguous 48 states, except for the high plains and Great Lakes region. The number overwintering depends on the severity of the winter.

Ask just about anyone to name five birds and this species will be one, it is so well known. It has rich brick red underparts, brownish gray back, black head with white eye ring and a deep yellow bill. The young are heavily spotted. The eastern subspecies tends to be richer in color and some northern forms have solid black backs.

This species occurs in just about every habitat, from coniferous forest to low desert and from high mountain to city yards. The nest is a strong, deep cup-like structure with mud lining and grass and leaf outsides wedged firmly in a tree crotch. It is often seen as it hops about the lawn, stops, cocks its head and pulls up a large worm.

If you have a yard, the robin will appear at some point! However, certain plants will particularly attract them. Berries of honeysuckle, bittersweet, sumac and especially cherry are sure to be visited. A mulberry tree can be the center of attraction until the berries are gone. In the winter in the north, apples placed out are excellent and sunflower seeds will also be taken. In southern sections such as Florida where incredible numbers spend the winter, pest species such as Brazilian pepper are fed on heavily.

Nesting platforms can be placed on sides of buildings or directly on tree trunks. A flat tray with a 6 in square base and small lip around it and with a roof or canopy for weather protection will often do the trick, but any flat surface with protection may be chosen. When people think of American birds, this is one of the first to come to mind. It certainly is comfortable living with people. A birdbath is one of the best items you can place out to hold these birds in an area, summer and winter.

FACTS AND FEATURES

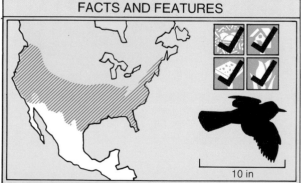

10 in

Plumage Bright rusty red breast; dark head; brownish gray back; yellow bill.
Habitat Everywhere! Forests, fields, parks, orchards, backyards. Mountain glades to coastal areas.
Food Earthworms, grubs, larvae, insects, spiders. In fall, berries and other fruit and seeds.

Nest A mud lined cup with grasses and rootlets. Placed on a flat surface: ledge of building, rock face, tree crotch, nesting shelter.

LOGGERHEAD SHRIKE *Lanius ludovicianus*

THIS SPECIES IS FOUND in all the contiguous 48 states and central southern Canada in the summer. They winter mainly in Virginia, Missouri, south Utah and north California. In the north eastern portion of its range, this species has decreased dramatically in the last decade.

A grayish bird with black face mask, its rump is gray and wings black, as is the tail. The bill is small. The lookalike northern shrike has a very heavy bill, barring on the chest and a white rump. In the loggerhead the tail is not pumped up and down as we see in the northern. The song is an almost "electronic" mass of jumbled notes.

This shrike occurs in a wide range of habitats. In the north, it is found in open brushy fields and meadows, and in the south open farmlands. In the west a desert species exists in mesquite and cactus areas. In some places there seems to be a loggerhead for every stretch of powerline between poles! Typically it perches high, then drops down and with rapid wingbeats moves to another perch swooping up to settle. Hunting prey, it swoops down or plunges to capture insects, small mammals or even young birds. It nests in open areas, gardens and shrub fields. The nest is a loose mass of plant material (twigs, stems and rootlets) well lined with grasses and feathers. In some areas it may nest three times a year.

This is not a species you can set out to attract to a yard but is certainly one that is regularly encountered in the southern and western regions. It will visit the edge of clearings and may rest in open shrubby fields. In many southern areas nests can be found low down in garden shrubs. They need areas for impaling food, hence hawthorn shrub near a likely spot could be an attractant. The prey, whether insect or small mammal, is impaled on the barbs or thorns of a bush. Insects impaled in such a fashion are often the first sign that the species is present. In areas of limited food, this species may hold winter feeding territories like its larger northern relative.

FACTS AND FEATURES

Plumage A black and gray bird. Black wings and tail; white patches in wing; black face mask.

Habitat Open areas of all types, usually with shrubs. Farmland, prairies, deserts, fields, parks.

Food Larger insects such as locust, small mammals, small birds and their young.

Nest A bulky, rather flat structure of twigs, grasses, and plant stems. In dense brush or thicket.

9 in

Easily mistaken for a mockingbird because of the similar plumage color, the loggerhead can be distinguished by its short, hooked bill, black face mask and fast beating, undulating flight. Commonly impales prey on thorny twigs, thus forming a larder.

GRAY CATBIRD *Dumetella carolinensis*

THE GRAY CATBIRD IS an abundant summer resident east of a line running from western Washington through Wyoming to eastern Texas. Southern birds are permanent on their range and, depending on the severity of winters, few or many birds stay in the thickets in New England.

Often heard as it gives its cat-like *mewing* sound from a thicket, it is easily identified, being all dark gray in color with black cap and rusty undertail coverts. The black tail is often cocked at an upward angle.

This is a bird of the dense thickets, grapevine tangles and brush piles. It is certainly one of the most abundant summer species in the northeast. The nest is a bulky affair of twigs, grapevine strips and rootlet lining placed in a dense low bush such as a greenbrier or rose tangle. It is a fairly good mimic, and a jumble of songs as well as nasal and squeaky sequences proclaim the territory. The same areas used during the summer serve as a winter habitat for those birds that decide to stick out a cold northern winter.

A wide variety of plant food is taken. Blackberry ranks as a prime food item and cherry, elderberry, greenbrier mulberry, blueberry and pokeweed are all taken with relish. Plantings of any of these in or near a thicket area will certainly attract this species, and they will often bring their young to these bushes. As winter food, holly, bittersweet and honeysuckle are sure bets. Old apples will be pecked at and under extreme pressure gray catbirds will come for suet and peanut butter. Water is important as they are incessant bathers, be it in woodland streams or backyard birdbaths.

It could be said that of all native songbirds, fleshy fruits are almost the exclusive food source. Therefore, planting the right type of shrub can play an important role when trying to attract birds to stay over winter or to nest nearby.

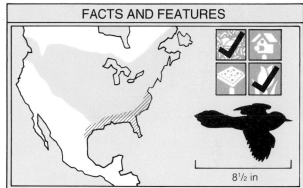

FACTS AND FEATURES

8½ in

Plumage Dark gray bird with black cap, black tail and rusty undertail coverts.
Habitat Forest understory, thickets, shrubby areas, riverine forest, gardens, backyards.
Food About 50 percent animal matter and 50 percent berries, fruits and seeds.

Nest A bulky affair of sticks, grasses, leaves. In the center a cup of rootlets, fibers and plant down.

Widespread, except in the more western states, the gray catbird acquired its name from its cat-like, mewing call. It prefers bushy habitats, especially wood margins and scrub in residential areas.

NORTHERN MOCKINGBIRD *Mimus polyglottos*

THIS SPECIES RANGES FROM NORTHERN California across Utah and on into the southern edge of North Dakota, on through to southern Maine, and south throughout the United States. The northern part of its range has extended dramatically, especially in the last decade. Scattered populations now appear in southern Canada. A correlation has been drawn in the east between the spread of the mockingbird and the dramatic expansion of range of the multiflora rose, one of its favorite food plants.

An all gray bird, it is darker above with a long, rounded, dark tail that flashes white on the outer edges in

108

flight. The wings, with two wing bars, exhibit large white patches when in flight. Some birds have a hint of a dark line running through the eye. Best known for its singing, it is an excellent mimic as the latin name implies. It mimics a wide range of species and has its own song which is rather musical and bubbling with an occasional chuck or harsh note thrown in. During the spring it often sings all night long.

A common bird in cities, gardens, field edges, open glades and desert regions, it can often be seen hunting the lawns, using wing-flashing and tail-spreading displays to chase up insects. For nesting it retires to thickets where its bulky rather flat nest is tucked into a tangle. In desert areas cacti are used for nesting. In areas of consistent weather, three nestings are not uncommon.

Providing a sheltered area, such as a dense woodpile, is one step you can take to attract this species directly to your area. More than likely the species is present in the near vicinity. It hunts opne areas such as lawns but relies on dense cover for nesting. Birdbaths are a great attraction.

In the northern sections where there are harsh winters, the birds will come to feeding stations. They take oilseeds and peanut hearts, often storing them in an abandoned nest in a nearby thicket which will be "their thicket" for the winter. Holly, hackberry, sumac and Virginia creeper are good winter foods. Summer food includes blackberries, mulberry, grape and pokeweed. As mentioned above, multiflora rose has provided the food source for range extension in some areas. However, it has a tendency to overrun large areas, and if planted in a yard as an attractant could generate too much trouble.

FACTS AND FEATURES

11 in

Plumage Large, long tailed gray bird with large white wing patches and white outer tail feathers.
Habitat Gardens, farmlands, parks, backyards. Any brushy second growth area. Multiflora rose a key shrub.
Food Wild berries (rose hips) seeds, insects, invertebrates.

Nest Large structure of twigs, grasses and rootlets placed in dense shrubbery. In desert areas in cacti tangles.

The long, slender bill coupled with grayish plumage, white on wings and outer tail feathers easily identify the northern mockingbird (left). In flight, the slow wing beats clearly show the conspicuous white wing patches.

This bird (left) with its very erect posture, and cocked tail, is showing very little white in the wing — probably due to wear on the feathers. The bird at the nest (right) is far more typical. The nest, too, is typical: placed in a small tree and consisting of a bulky cup of twigs and grasses, lined with finer materials. Three to five eggs are usual, and although the nest is built by both adults, only the female incubates the eggs. Both adults feed the young which leave the nest after 12-14 days.

BROWN THRASHER *Toxostoma rufum*

The brown upperparts and streaked underparts of the brown thrasher resemble the wood thrush, but its larger size, long tail, double white wing bars and long, decurved bill distinguish it. The eye is yellow in adult birds, gray or brown in immatures.

THIS SPECIES RANGES FROM central southern Canada south to eastern Texas and eastward to the coast. It is a summer resident in the northern portion of this range and permanent from Virginia and Kentucky to Oklahoma (except in the Appalachians).

It is rich foxy brown above and heavily streaked below. Two wing bars are obvious. The bill is dark and the tail very long. The eye is yellow, and is sometimes tinted with orange. The song is distinctive—a variety of musical to harsh phrases, sung in couplets.

A bird of the undergrowth and thickets it is not usually found in deep woods, preferring gardens, weed fields, lot edges and hedgerows normally quite close to human habitation. The singing perch is often high atop a tree in the nesting area but the nest itself is placed down near the ground in dense cover. Their presence is often detected as they scratch about the leaves of the thicket floor. Often very intent on this work, they will allow a close approach before hopping off or darting away flashing the rufous color. A good deal of their time is spent directly on the ground searching through the leaf litter.

Depending on the severity of the winter, few or numerous individuals will stay in the northern regions. Staying in thickets, they may venture to the edge of feeding areas to take sunflower seeds and will occasionally be bold enough to go for suet. During the breeding season brush piles are an attractant as is a

birdbath or expanse of water. For plantings, blackberries are a favorite item as are elderberries, mulberries, holly and hackberry. If cover is provided and there are berries available, this species adapts well to coming into yards and gardens. A simple hedgerow is often enough.

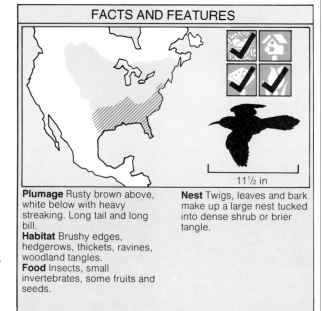

FACTS AND FEATURES

11½ in

Plumage Rusty brown above, white below with heavy streaking. Long tail and long bill.
Habitat Brushy edges, hedgerows, thickets, ravines, woodland tangles.
Food Insects, small invertebrates, some fruits and seeds.

Nest Twigs, leaves and bark make up a large nest tucked into dense shrub or brier tangle.

CEDAR WAXWING *Bombycilla cedrorum*

THIS SPECIES BREEDS THROUGHOUT most of Canada, and in the United States the population spreads down the west coast to southern California. Missing in the Sierra Nevada, the population then spreads east across north Colorado, is scattered through the Mississippi valley and then spreads out on the east coast from the southern tip of the Appalachians in Georgia north through Maine and on to the coast. In winter, birds from the north stay throughout the remaining southern parts of the United States, often in incredible numbers.

A silky smooth bird of warm browns and subtle grays, it has a black mask which runs through the eye while the head is topped by a distinct crest. The tail tip is bright yellow and the brilliant waxy tips to the secondaries (which gives the species its name) shows prominently in the wing. Young birds are heavily streaked below with brown but have the black mask and yellow tail tip.

This bird moves about in large groups outside the nesting season. It frequents a wide range of habitat and can be expected just about anywhere from farmland to city parks. It nests in open areas or at the fringes of woodlands and along creeks. Nesting often occurs late in the year when berries are available for young. They have a split preference for food—during the winter taking berries, switching to insects in the spring and back to berries in the fall. During insect hatches they can often be seen darting out over ponds and lakes, as well as river courses and fields, acting like flycatchers in pursuit of prey. They grab an individual before darting back to their perch. Large flocks are often involved in such hunts.

Though they do not come to bird feeders they are readily attracted by plantings. Numerous plants provide winter food as well as food during nesting periods. Some favorites are pyracantha, mountain ash, mulberry, red cedar juniper, cherry and dogwood. Chokecherry, elderberry and the like are also widely consumed. It is not uncommon to find a flock of birds feeding on overripe berries and becoming intoxicated to the point where they can be picked up. In a short time this wears off and they go about their business.

Making food available for long periods and also providing overwinter food supplies can be a most effective attraction. Water should also be made available. Though unpredictable in their wanderings, these facilities are sure to attract flocks of cedar waxwings at some time.

The cedar is distinguished from the bohemian waxwing by its smaller size, yellow belly, white undertail coverts and lack of white or yellow in the wing. Juveniles have a short crest and are much grayer than adults; they lack the black on the throat and have little or no red tips to the secondaries.

FACTS AND FEATURES

7 in

Plumage Soft looking, light brown and gray upperparts and chest. Crest, black mask through eye. Red waxy tips on secondaries; yellow terminal tail band.
Habitat Open woodland, brushy open areas, secondary growth zones. It is a wanderer; parks and gardens when moving.

Food Diet mainly of berries and seeds but will switch to insects when plentiful.
Nest Neat cup of grasses, rootlets, bark strips placed in a dense bush or shrub.

WHITE-EYED VIREO *Vireo griseus*

THE RANGE OF THE WHITE-EYED VIREO encompasses an area from Connecticut west through the Great Lakes region to northern Missouri, and then south through mid-Texas. The northern edge of the range is slowly extending each year. Birds in Florida and the Gulf Coast are permanent on their range.

They are usually first detected by an explosive call from the thicket, a distinctive *chick-a-pu-wheer—chick*. They are readily attracted by a *squeak* noise, and will respond with harsh scolds and raspy notes. Usually they can be seen peering through an opening in the thicket. Gray above with white wing bars, yellow tinted on the undersides, they have a distinctive yellow circle around the eye and out to the bill. The eye itself is white.

A skulker in the thickets, it is usually found quite close to the ground and is distinctly shy except when singing on its territory during the breeding season. Their habitat preference is dense thickets of moist, swamp areas but thickets of any sort, as long as they are dense, will do. In the southern swampland and bayou country this species is abundant. The nest is a pendulant cup suspended from a fork in a thicket shrub. It is made of plant stalks and fibers and covered with fibrous material.

The best that can be done to attract this species is to allow thickets and underbrush to remain in place, especially if greenbrier tangles are within the complex. Brush piles also offer cover especially during winter months in southern areas. Though insects make up the majority of their diet, berries are also taken. Waxmyrtle, holly, elderberry, poison ivy, sassafrass and Virginia creeper have all been found to be part of the complex. Dense thickets of honeysuckle offer cover and berries.

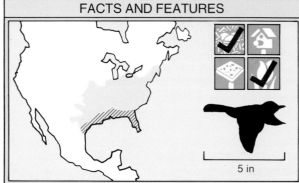

FACTS AND FEATURES

Plumage Bright yellow "spectacles"; white eye in adults; gray crown and back; yellow flanks; gray white underbelly.
Habitat Thickets, brier tangles, swampy areas, canebrakes, dense forest undergrowth.

Food Insects of all types, spiders and other invertebrates; some berries.
Nest Pendulant structure in limb crotch made of bark strips, grasses, and plant fibers. Covered with spider web, mosses and some lichen.

One of the smaller vireos, the white-eyed has olive green upperparts, a head washed with gray, and whitish underparts tinged with yellow on the sides. It has two wing bars and a yellow line from bill to eye and around eye. The diagnostic white eye can be seen only at close quarters.

RED-EYED VIREO *Vireo olivaceus*

THIS SPECIES IS COMMON TO ABUNDANT throughout the eastern half of North America to a line running roughly from south Washington east to mid-Nebraska and south through eastern Texas. In winter they migrate south into Central and South America.

It is a trim vireo with an olive green back, dark gray cap and a white line over the eye offset by black lines bordering the top and bottom of this line. The underparts are grayish to light white. In first year birds the underparts often have a yellowish tint to the lower belly. The eye is bright red in adults and dark in immatures. On occasion the yellow underbellied "yellow-green" vireo strays into southern Texas. This is now considered a subspecies.

The song is a repetitive series in a "question answer" repetition. Noted as being one of the most continuous of songsters, the song can be heard from sunrise to sunset, even in the heat of midday! It is a typical sound of the upland woods of eastern North America.

This species is encountered rather than attracted. If your grounds have tall trees with significant undergrowth, chances are this bird will appear there at some time during the breeding season or migration.

The nest, a fiber-covered pendulant cup, is placed in the fork of a branch usually quite low to the ground. These "gray" nests are a familiar sight in the winter woodlands. Deciduous upland woods are the favorite habitat so if these are available this species will certainly be seen. Almost exclusively an insect eater, only in the hardest of times will it take berries, and then just to store energy to migrate elsewhere. Virginia creeper, spicebush and sumac are three berries they have been seen to take.

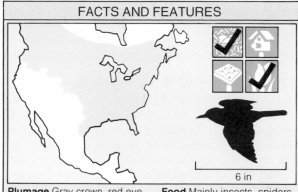

FACTS AND FEATURES

Plumage Gray crown, red eye in adults. Olive brown back; white line over eye bordered by black top and bottom; no wing bars; green underparts.
Habitat Second growth woodlands with shrubby understory, open woods, parks, orchards, swamps.

Food Mainly insects, spiders, other invertebrates. Some berries and seeds.
Nest A well woven cup of plant fibers and grasses, covered with spider web and some lichens. Pendulant from fork of outer shrub branches.

6 in

One of the largest vireos with no wing bars. The red eye is not always easy to see in the field. In southeast Texas a separate race occurs which is grayer above, has bright yellow on the underparts and indistinct black lines on the head.

ORANGE-CROWNED WARBLER *Vermivora celata*

DURING THE BREEDING SEASON this species is strictly a western inhabitant. It breeds along the entire west coast from Alaska south through California, across Canada, down the Rockies and throughout Washington and Idaho south through Nevada into California. It is one of the warblers that winters in the United States in a narrow band running from the Carolinas south to Florida, west along the Gulf Coast and the southern part of Texas. A thin winter population hangs on in the extreme west coast region from south Washington to south California and through Arizona. Scattered birds winter as far north as New England.

Considered by many field guides as the drabest of the warblers, its rich yellowish underparts contrast with the deep olive green of the back. There is an eyeline, and the yellow tinted undertail coverts are also yellow. Several races occur with varying shades of underpart yellow. The crown is a tawny orange.

A bird of open brush areas, thick undergrowth of woodland edges, hedgerows and thickets, it confines most of its activities there, rarely venturing higher than 15 ft off the ground. They attract readily to squeaking and their presence is detected by a loud metallic chip.

The nest is placed on the ground in the extreme northern portions of its range (it nests to tree limit) whereas in the southern areas it is more commonly placed low down in a dense bush. The cup-like nest is made of plant material and is often lined with fur or feathers.

This is one of the few warblers that actually come to feeding stations. It may take oil-seed sunflower and will certainly feed heavily on suet. It also takes Eleagnus berries, poison ivy and will peck at honeysuckle when short of food in a northern winter. Providing ample cover via brush piles or allowing understory thickets to establish themselves is one way to attract visiting birds. It will certainly be used during migration for cover.

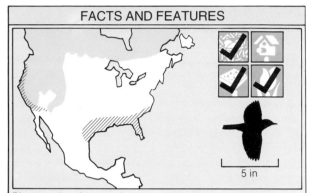

FACTS AND FEATURES

5 in

Plumage A uniform grayish green to yellowish green with faint streaking on breast and sides. Orange crown on male usually hidden by other feathers.
Habitat Brushy areas, thicketed hillsides, chapparal, coniferous woods blended with aspens, forest edges.

Food Mainly insects and spiders but in fall will take seeds and small berries.
Nest Built low to ground or on the ground. Made of grasses, bark strips and plant down.

The longer tail and thinner, decurved bill separate this bird from Tennessee warbler. The dull orange crown patch is partly concealed and not always easy to see in the field. The song is a trill, slowing at the end. While some birds are bright yellow on the underparts, other races are noticeably gray.

YELLOW-THROATED WARBLER *Dendroica dominica*

THIS SPECIES RANGES FROM the Pennsylvania line and mid-New Jersey, south through Florida, west to mid-Texas and Oklahoma, through middle Missouri and Indiana. It is a permanent resident from South Carolina south as well as in a thin belt along the Gulf Coast.

A handsome warbler with blue gray back, it has a black mask through the eye, white eye line, rich lemon yellow throat and black side streaks. The underparts are pure white. A white neck patch is located to the rear of the black mask.

This is a bird of forests and swamplands. Though a good deal of its time is spent foraging in the upper canopy of trees, they do sometimes come down to the lower outer tips of limbs. A variety of trees attract their attention—cypress, pine, oak and sycamore (indeed, at one point they had the common name of sycamore warbler). When winter populations shift south they appear en masse in a variety of vegetation. In peak migration mornings palm trees in particular can be seen literally dripping with this species.

The nest, a cup of plant material, plant fibers, cobwebs and bark, is placed in dense clumps of Spanish moss when available. In the northern areas, where there is no moss, the nest is placed on a limb usually quite high above the ground. In spring and fall migration periods this species often appears far to the north and west of its usual range.

Migrants are more than likely to show up in any patch of woods or garden especially if Spanish moss (which plays a vital role in the placement of nests in the south) is present.

Wintering populations are attracted to insects drawn into fruits and may even take a little fruit for themselves. Seeds at feeding trays have been taken but this really is an emergency food supply. Very active and confiding, migrant birds may literally feed within touch on a lawn or within a thicket, especially on wintering grounds.

FACTS AND FEATURES

5½ in

Plumage Unmarked blue gray back; brilliant yellow throat; black eye patch with white line above. White underparts and streaked sides.
Habitat Pine woods, cypress swamps, palm groves, oak forest. Prefers areas with Spanish moss.

Food Mainly insects and spiders. Little fruit taken in fall and winter.
Nest A cup of grasses, plant fibers, plant down and spider web placed in Spanish moss clump or in tree crotch.

The white neck patch and plain gray back separate the yellow-throated from the similar Grace's warbler. The whitish eye stripe, neck patch and double wing bars, coupled with black face, yellow breast and black streaks on white underparts make this a most handsome bird. The female has less black on the crown.

115

YELLOW WARBLER *Dendroica petechia*

ONE OF THE MOST WIDESPREAD of all the warblers, this species ranges from Alaska through Canada and throughout the lower 48 states except for Texas, the margin of the Gulf Coast states and Florida. However, it can be seen in these areas during migration periods. The species winters in Mexico, and a small year-round population can be found in extreme south California and Arizona.

FACTS AND FEATURES

Plumage Brilliant yellow to orange yellow, with fine reddish breast streaks; jet black eye. Female: pale yellow.
Habitat Wet habitats, open woodlands, parkland, orchards. Willows preferred.

Food Mainly insects at all stages of development; some spiders; other invertebrates. Some berries.
Nest A fine built cup of plant fibers, grasses and down, covered with willow threads and spider web. Placed in a crotch of a smaller tree.

A brilliant yellow to orange-yellow bird, it has an olive yellow back, rusty red beak and belly streaks. The button-like eye is pure black. The female is dull yellow and olive with a jet black eye and possibly faint breast streaks.

A bird of many habitats, wet meadows are certainly a preferred location especially if its favorite tree, the willow, is present. They also frequent woodlots, open woods, powerlines, orchards and gardens. In migration they appear everywhere. A constant singer, they are active in territory defense and can be seen darting from one bush to another during courtship periods.

The nest is a beautiful structure. Placed in the crotch of a tree, it is made of plant fibers and grasses and then covered with willow strips and gray plant fiber. Nests are heavily parasitized by cowbirds in some areas. At times the female recognizes the egg is not hers and builds a new floor over the egg and increases the sides of the nest in height. In some cases two of these chambers have been found in an active nest.

This species will very often visit a garden or backyard during migration. Nesting may occur if proper shrub areas are nearby. The yard often becomes a site for the parent bird to forage for food. While no specific foods attract this species—their diet consists exclusively of insects—water is one of the best attractions for all warblers. This can be a birdbath, pool-like depression or an elaborate running water system. The sound of water dripping is often more attractive to this species than a birdbath. A system as simple as a suspended bucket with a hole in it which allows the water to drip slowly should suffice. The sound of the water "plunking" on a rock below will attract the bird's attention, and if the dripping water collects in a basin at the rock's edge, bathing and drinking are sure to take place. If the species is seen frequenting your yard during the nesting season, an onion bag with cotton protruding can attract attention and may be used as nesting material.

A dumpy warbler with a short tail and a dark eye, the plumage of the yellow warbler is striking, especially in the male, who is brighter and also has reddish streaks on breast and underparts. Yellow spots on the tail are diagnostic. The clear song consists of several sweet notes, zwee zwee zwee, but it can vary.

YELLOW-RUMPED WARBLER *Dendroica coronata*

THIS SPECIES RANGES THROUGHOUT Alaska and Canada, and in the southwest Washington and Montana to south California and New Mexico. In the east, the breeding range is confined to New York, New England and sections around the Great Lakes. The winter range is extensive, from southern New England south through Florida and southwest of the Great Lakes to western Texas.

Perhaps the commonest warbler of North America, two types are now identifiable after having been considered separate species for many years—the "audubon" form and the "myrtle" form. Myrtles have blue gray backs, bright yellow rumps, a yellow shoulder patch and golden yellow crown. The throat is white. The female is brownish with a white underbelly. It is yellow in the same places as the male with the exception of the crown. The audubon type has a deep yellow throat and lacks the black eye patch of the myrtle. Western birds are mainly audubons, and eastern birds mainly myrtles.

Mixed deciduous and conifers form the breeding habitat. The cup-like nest of plant material, covered with fibers, lichens and moss, is placed in a crotch or astride a limb and can be anything from 5 to 50 ft up! In many areas this species is called the "spider bird" due to its habit of working in and around buildings, stealing insects from the webs and picking off random spiders on the building surface. Though they usually nest in mature forests, large trees in and around buildings often attract the birds and they adapt well to living near human habitation.

It is difficult to establish a set program to attract this species. However, plantings and trees on the ground are certain to provide the type of environment that they prefer. In the winter months at the northern part of the range several berries form the bulk of their diet. Patches of these plants can attract the birds and play an important part in their feeding. The preferred plants are: sumac, bayberry (hence the name for the eastern form—myrtle), and red cedar juniper.

♂

Two distinct races, once thought to be separate species occur. The northeastern form, the myrtle has white sides of neck, throat and line above eye, while the western or audubon form has a yellow throat. All females are duller. Both forms have white spots on the tail. The song is a soft, trilling warble.

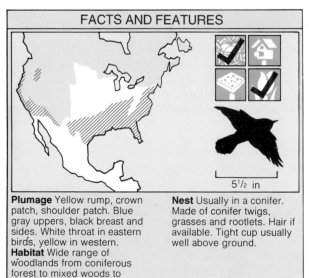

FACTS AND FEATURES

Plumage Yellow rump, crown patch, shoulder patch. Blue gray uppers, black breast and sides. White throat in eastern birds, yellow in western.
Habitat Wide range of woodlands from coniferous forest to mixed woods to deciduous forest.
Food Spiders, insects, berries, fruits and seeds.

Nest Usually in a conifer. Made of conifer twigs, grasses and rootlets. Hair if available. Tight cup usually well above ground.

5½ in

117

BLACK AND WHITE WARBLER *Mniotilta varia*

The main characteristics of this warbler are its plumage and its habit of feeding on tree trunks or branches, moving around like a nuthatch. It is the only warbler with a black and white plumage that has a white stripe through the crown. The song is a high, thin, rolling weet-see, weet-see.

A BIRD PREDOMINANTLY OF the eastern half of North America where deciduous forests occur, it is lacking from the Great Plains but occurs in woodlands from the Dakotas south through Texas. The east coast breeding range terminates in south Georgia. Wintering birds can be found in the southern tip of Florida or around the Gulf Coast to the tip of Texas.

One of the easiest of the warblers to identify, it has a striking black and white pattern. The male has a black cheek and throat and black undertail markings. This bird searches trunks and limbs of trees in "nuthatch" fashion, often hanging upside down beneath limbs. There is a white stripe down the center of the crown which the similar-looking blackpoll lacks.

A bird of mixed deciduous conifer woodlands, it is one of the more abundant warblers and also one of the first to arrive in the northern part of its range. This is because it gleans trunks and limbs for insects' eggs and larvae and does not need the insect population of the leafy canopy. The nest is most often placed in a depression at the base of a large tree and very likely in a wet area. On one occasion a nest was found inside a dead tree stump, tucked under an overhanging piece of wood.

Though not really a species that attracts to a yard, it may be encountered there or in parks and gardens usually in migration. In wintering areas it occasionally comes to a feeder, where suet is the item that is sought. A swampy area at the edge of a forested region may attract this species to nest and this handsome warbler is often seen in large trees and gardens.

FACTS AND FEATURES

5¼ in

Plumage Striking black and white streaks. Male has black cheek.
Habitat Open deciduous woods, swamplands and mixed woodland. In migration, occurs in any habitat.
Food Insects, eggs, larvae, pupae; spiders gleaned from trunk and limb crevices.

Nest Usually at the base of a tree on the ground. Of leaves and grasses, often with a canopy.

AMERICAN REDSTART *Setophaga ruticilla*

DURING THE SUMMER this species ranges from New England south to Georgia, west to the edge of the plains of Oklahoma, Nebraska and Iowa then on to the northwest as far as eastern Washington. It is found across Canada and just reaches the panhandle of Alaska.

The male is jet black with orange markings at the shoulder, wings and tail base. The female is olive-backed with a grayish head, white below with yellow in the wing, shoulder and tail base. It takes two years for the male to acquire adult plumage, and so males returning in their first spring have patches of orange and flecks of black showing through. They are constantly on the move, often hopping along a branch swinging the whole body from one side to the other in a zigzag fashion. The tail is rapidly fanned showing the diagnostic orange or yellow squares at the sides of the base. They also "flutter" feed, dropping from a branch, fluttering beneath a leaf or falling through the air fluttering and capturing insects while flaring their wings as they twist from side to side.

This is a common species of secondary growth woodlands. It also favors swampy areas and new growth hillsides. Mixed woodlands and coniferous zones are also used but not with the same abundance of the secondary growth areas. During migrations the sheer numbers of this species encountered in a day is often overwhelming.

The nest, a beautiful cup of fibers, bark strips, grasses and covered with cobwebs and lichens, is placed securely in the fork of a sapling. While usually placed near to the ground the nest can, on rare occasions, be as high as 20 ft.

Keeping a dense undergrowth in a woodlot or allowing saplings to remain is a step in the right direction toward providing nesting habitat. Water is also an attractant for all warblers. During migration, even if there is only one tree on a property, there is a good chance this species will appear at some point. In gardens and orchards these birds often find such good insect hunting that they spend several days in one locality and at times in one tree. In the winter a small population can be found in the southern tip of Florida but remain in the scrub rather than coming to a feeder situation.

Extremely active, this bird darts after flying insects. In flight, and while flicking its wings and tail when perched, the male's orangy patches on the wings and tail flash conspicuously against the black plumage. The females are grayish olive above with yellow patches on the wings and tail.

♀

♂

FACTS AND FEATURES

5 in

Plumage Male: shiny black with brilliant orange patches at shoulder, wing and tail. Female: gray back with yellow at shoulder wing and tail.
Habitat Deciduous woodlands with scrub and thicket understory. Gardens and parks with shrub and young tree growth.

Food Insects; often flying forms and spiders. Some fruits and seeds.
Nest Beautiful elongated cup of plant fibers and rootlets bound by spider web. Often lined with hair or very fine grass, in shrub crotch.

COMMON YELLOWTHROAT *Geothlypis trichas*

♀

♂

The male of this species is distinguished by its black face mask and yellow throat making it one of the easiest birds to identify. The female's face is dark olive, but the throat is also yellow. Western birds have more yellow on the underparts than eastern birds and the birds of the southwest are the brightest of all forms.

AN ABUNDANT SPECIES THROUGHOUT the lower 48 states and all but northern Canada and Alaska, the common yellowthroat remains as a permanent resident in the southern part of the United States.

The male is unmistakable, with yellow underparts, brown back and a jet black face mask bordered on the top with a bluish white. Females are brown backed, with gray cheeks and rich yellow underparts that run right up the throat to the bill. Depending on the geographic area where encountered, the extent of yellow on the underparts does vary. The song is a distinctive repetitive *wichity, wichity, wichity.* The call note a harsh, sharp *check.* It often keeps the tail cocked like a wren.

The favored habitat is moist open areas such as wet fields and swamps. Even the smallest cattail pocket will often harbor a pair of these birds. Dense thickets and shrubby areas are also attractive. In migration nearly any thicket will produce this species. Occasionally during these migration periods they will even forage for insects in the top of large trees. But by and large they spend their life within a few feet of the ground. The nest is placed within a few feet of the ground or on the ground in dryer conditions. The nest is made up of a cup of grasses, leaves, bark strips and plant fibers, and often has a canopy effect over from the backside. At times the interior will be lined with animal hair.

Like other warblers, it is mainly encountered in migration. However, if a property has a small wet area, a resident pair may establish themselves. Thicket edges along clearings, hedgerows and brush piles may also be used during the summer. Any supply of drinking water will be frequented during movement periods.

FACTS AND FEATURES

5 in

Plumage Olive brown back with pure yellow below from throat to undertail. Black face mask in male. Cocks tail like wren.
Habitat Damp fields, dense thickets, cattail marshes, swamplands, riverine thickets. Both fresh and salt water areas. Mangroves in south.

Food Insects in all stages of development.
Nest Built on or close to the ground. It is rather large and made of grasses, large leaves, bark strips; often cone shaped if in low shrub base.

Blue Grosbeak *Guiraca caerulea*

THE BLUE GROSBEAK RANGES from central New Jersey west through central Illinois up to South Dakota south of Wyoming and then west through northern California, south to the coasts and Mexican border.

With a large bunting, it is a deep blue color offset by a black face mask and rich chestnut wing bars. The female is tawny brown with slightly lighter underparts. The bill is very heavy. The chestnut wing bars can be seen on a brownish wing background. The song is a sweet melody of jumbled notes in an oscillating pattern. One distinct tendency of this species is a rapid spreading and closing of the tail.

This is a bird of roadside thickets, scrub areas, overgrown weed fields and farmlands that have gone to weed in the fall. Hedgerows are also favored. They seem to favor sitting on power lines and fencing wires and the male will sing for extended periods of time from these perches. The nest is a fairly bulky cup of loose twigs, rootlets, and plant material from nearby crops (cotton, corn leaves etc.) and is lined with horsehair or other fine grasses and materials. Often shed snakeskins are included in the nest, a habit shared with a few other birds including the crested flycatchers. During periods of migrations they disperse far beyond the northern limits of their range. Very few birds spend the winter in the confines of the United States.

Brush piles are certainly a favored spot for this species. Particularly piles of bulky size and loose stature. Also weed patches left to develop can be excellent feeding areas and planting such as blackberry can provide adequate cover. The massive seed cracking bill points to the fact, that at a feeder, seeds are the only interest. Like their northern relatives, sunflower seeds are the favorite. In the wheat growing and corn belt areas of the country, these crops are the preferred food source. Grass seeds make up the bulk of this species diet.

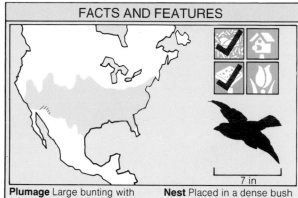

FACTS AND FEATURES

Plumage Large bunting with deep blue plumage; wide rusty wing bars. Black mask at bill base. Female is brownish. Immatures can be almost orange in color.
Habitat Woodland edges, river thickets, weed fields.
Food Seeds, berries and other fruit. Insects, spiders, egg cases and larvae.

Nest Placed in a dense bush the nest is bulky and made of roots, grasses, twigs, plant stems, bark strips. Often snakeskin is incorporated, and in city areas plastic strips are worked into the base.

7 in

The larger size and rich, chestnut, double wing bars distinguish males from the indigo bunting. The female is also separable by size, bill shape and the presence of wing bars. These wing bars also separate it from the brown-headed cowbird in poor light. It frequently flicks or spreads its tail when perched.

♀

♂

NORTHERN CARDINAL *Cardinalis cardinalis*

THIS SPECIES IS A PERMANENT RESIDENT throughout its range. This range has extended northward dramatically over the last 20 years. From central Maine and even New Brunswick, south through Florida and west to the Dakotas, the edge of Colorado and throughout most of Texas. The Mexican population "creeps" over the New Mexican and Arizona border.

The male is unmistakable—a brilliant red bird with a crest and black face mask and bib. The female also has a crest and is a buffy brown tinted with red. A blackish face mask is outlined and the tail and wings are reddish. The bill is pink.

Throughout its rapidly expanding range, this is a common species. Warm mornings are accentuated by the rich whistled song, a loud and ringing *whit-tuuuu, whit-tuuu, cherr, cherr, cherr*. They are a common backyard species and have endeared themselves to all who have a pair or more coming to their feeders. They inhabit woodland edges, swamplands, thickets of parks, gardens, hedgerows, indeed any area where there is undergrowth cover. The nest is a bulky cup of grasses, bark, plant fibers, and rootlets placed in a dense shrub. The young are often taken to feeding stations and "introduced" to their winter "feeding grounds." In the spring the male is very attentive to the female, and at feeders, the offering of food is a common part of the bonding ritual.

Proper planting, cover, water and food availability can make this species a year-round resident in your yard. Make sure a birdbath or water in some form is available. Cover, be it a hedgerow, dense shrubs such as arborvitae,

FACTS AND FEATURES

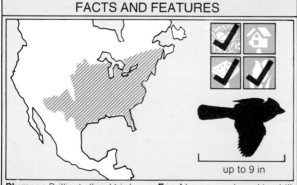

up to 9 in

Plumage Brilliant all red bird with a crest and black face mask. Female is soft brown also with a crest. Pink tints to plumage.
Habitat Backyard thickets, garden parks, farmland, overgrown fields, woodland edge.

Food Large seed cracking bill indicates its preference for seeds and fruits. Some insects, spiders and invertebrates.
Nest A loose cup of twigs, bark, grasses lined with fine grass or hair. Placed in dense shrubs or tangles.

or constructed brush piles are ideal. A wide variety of flowering trees and shrubs is also an attraction. Dogwoods, holly, pyracantha, and mulberry are all favorites. Pokeweed, blackberry, elderberry and sumac are all preferred foods.

At the feeding station it is best to feed on the ground. They rarely adapt to a window ledge but will come up to low feeding trays. On the ground, the seed can be spread over a larger area. This is especially important if you want to attract more than one pair. They are often very defensive of their winter food and if fed in a restricted area, only one pair will visit. Also remember to clean up sunflower husks in the spring. They will poison grass and prevent its growth! Sunflower is practically the exclusive favorite of the cardinal. Although mixed seeds can be put out, it is sunflower that they want. In fact, sunflowers can be grown and the large heads layed out in the feeding area. The birds will come to pluck out their own seeds. Their adapability to living in a backyard situation coupled with their brilliant color has made this one of the best loved songbirds of North America.

The male (above) is unmistakable; the overall red plumage, conspicuous crest, black face and throat with reddish conical bill easily distinguish it. The female (left) could, together with immatures, be confused with the pyrrhuloxia in the southwest, but the bill shape and color should help to distinguish it. The immature cardinals have dark brownish bills, are browner overall than adults, and immature females lack red in the plumage. It is a common garden visitor if water and berry-bearing bushes are provided. It also eats seeds, especially sunflower seeds, on the ground. It is an aggressive species which can prevent others from visiting the feeding station.

♂

ROSE-BREASTED GROSBEAK *Pheucticus ludovicianus*

THIS SPECIES INHABITS THE NORTHEAST portion of North America. They range from the Appalachians north into New England on into Canada, and also throughout the Great Lakes region and westward to central Oklahoma, Nebraska and the eastern portion of the Dakotas. In the winter they are exceptionally rare as an overwintering form.

With a massive seed cracking bill this bird is easily told by its size. The male is quite distinctive with a black and white pattern and rich rose throat patch. The wing linings are also rose and the rump pure white. In the first spring returning males have not acquired full plumage color and arc brownish above and with a "faded" throat color. The female looks like a large sparrow, brown above, heavily streaked underparts and with yellow wing linings. The head is dark brown with a white eye and crown stripes. The song is sweet and quite robin-like in quality. In the fall a squeaking *eek* call first indicates the bird's presence.

This is a bird of the open woodland with shrubby undergrowth and this type of habitat is widespread from city parks to rural roadsides. Wet areas and swamplands also have this type of habitat and are favored areas. Because they are birds of the tree tops, they are thought to be rare. Not so, indeed once you are familiar with the song or the diagnostic squeaky call, it is obvious that they are quite common. The nest is a loose, flat structure mainly constructed of small twigs with some leaves and plant stems. Often it is so loosely constructed the incubating bird can be seen on the nest from below. In most of the range they are double brooded with the female incubating the second clutch, while the male cares for the first fledglings.

Fruiting trees and shrubs of many sorts are attractive to this species. In the spring, they visit cherry trees in blossom and feed on the pistil base of the flower. Elderberry is another favorite. Indeed, most of the trees in spring attract attention. Later on, dogwood berries, pokewood, beech and chokecherry are all taken with relish. With bills capable of cracking cherry pits, no fruit is too difficult for them to open. Birdbaths seem to be a favored spot for migrants or nearby nesting birds. Wintering birds are too rare to be expected but when they do occur like their northern cousins, sunflower seeds are also an exclusive food.

FACTS AND FEATURES

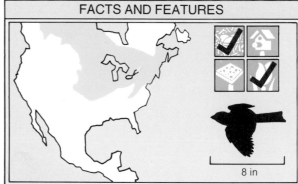

8 in

Plumage Large finch with very heavy bill. Male: black head and back; rose-red breast; white rump and wing patches. Female: soft brown with streaked head.
Habitat Open deciduous woodlands, parks, orchards, backyards.

Food About 50/50 insects and fruit. In winter possibly attracted to fruit and seeds. Loves cherry blossoms in spring.
Nest A loose shallow cup of twigs, grasses and rootlets, high in a deciduous tree.

The adult male is easily identified by its combination of black and white upperparts, white wing patches and bright rose-red breast patch contrasing with white underparts. In flight, the rose-red wing linings also show from below. The female resembles the female purple finch, but is larger, has a pale line through the crown and a more massive bill.

♂

INDIGO BUNTING *Passerina cyanea*

Smaller than the blue grosbeak and with a much smaller bill, the indigo bunting lacks wing bars. Females may have some blue in the plumage, usually in the tail. Females and immatures are separated from sparrows by unstreaked backs. The song is long and consists of a series of paired notes which are very varied.

AS A SUMMER RESIDENT this species ranges through the eastern half of the United States, from the Dakotas south through mid-Texas to the Rio Grande Valley. A western extension leads through Wyoming, Nevada, south Utah and Arizona.

Although the male is a deep blue all over, in poor light it will appear dark gray or black in color. A small black area surrounds the base of the bill. The lower mandible is white. The female is a rich tawny brown, darker on the back. The throat is pale. Males in transition from the blue summer pattern to the drab brown of winter are often odd looking with their mix of blue coloration.

They are a common bird of second growth areas, woodland edges, orchards, parks and garden plots. The key to attracting them is the young age of plants in the area. In many sections of the United States this species has benefited from power line clearings. These areas are continuously manicured to a steady state of secondary growth and the populations of birds are booming.

The male is a consistent singer and sings not only throughout the day but also longer into the year than most other summer species. It terminates prolonged songs in mid-August. The nest is a well made structure of grasses, vines, leaves and rootlets usually placed low down in a shrub fork.

They depart the United States almost totally in the winter except for a population that lingers in the extreme southern tip of Florida. Orchards are favored spots and if there is a chance of allowing secondary scrub growth on a property it increases the chances of this species occurring. Brush piles will also be frequented but are not as favored by this species as by others such as blue grosbeaks. Allowing a garden plot to run to full seed and winter weed in the fall is an excellent way to attract a myriad of fall seed eaters and this is the type of habitat most favored by indigos at that time of year.

FACTS AND FEATURES

5½ in

Plumage A small, deep blue bunting lacking wing bars. In some light it appears all black. The female is a warm brown.
Habitat Cut-over areas, re-growth burn sites, powerlines, weedy fields, orchards, parkland, open clearings.

Food During the summer, insects and spiders are almost the exclusive diet with many larvae taken. Seeds and some fruit may be taken.
Nest A shallow cup of twigs, leaves and plant fibers, placed in a dense brush tangle or low tree.

125

PAINTED BUNTING *Passerina ciris*

WITH A SPLIT RANGE IMAGE this bird can be found in a coastal population ranging from southern North Carolina to mid-Florida. And also a second population from the New Mexico border east as far as Missouri and south to Alabama and south of that line on through to Mexico. Winter populations can be found in southern Florida and along the Gulf Coast.

In a breeding plumage the male is considered one of the most striking birds in the United States. As a small bunting, it has a brilliant blue head, yellow green back and red underparts. The lower back and rump show brilliant red. The female is a lime green color, often tinting to gray green underparts.

This is a typical garden species in the range and also frequents roadside thickets, hedgerows, woodland edges, swampy land and edges of streams and rivers. They are shy birds and will usually flit off at the first sign of an intrusion. A low chipping or twittering note may be the only indication they are in a thicket. They will attract to squeaking to a degree but more often than not they will simply peer from deep position in the thicket and then slip away.

Feeding on grassy areas of roadside verges, they dart into the undercover before you get a good view. However, during mating season the male is often a tireless singer from a conspicuous perch. Wintering birds will come to the feeding tray. The nest is a deep cup in a fork of a tree or shrub woven with fine materials, such as grass, rootlets and plant fibers. The supports to the nest are encompassed with the nesting material.

Ample cover must be available before this bird will visit at any time of the year. Brush piles are excellent. Thick undercover plants, weedy areas, and dense hedgerow or evergreen will provide the needed protection. Though grass seeds form the bulk of the wild diet, at the feeding tray oil-seed sunflower is readily taken. Providing water in a sheltered spot is another attractant. Buckwheat, canary seed and thistle seed are also taken.

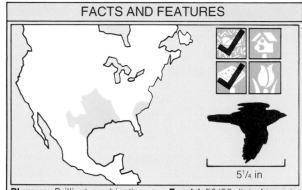

FACTS AND FEATURES

Plumage Brilliant combination of blue head, green back, bright red rump and underparts. Female a dark green above and yellowish below.

Habitat Fencerows, weedy thickets, field edges, brushy fields, shrubs and weeds along riverbanks.

Food A 50/50 diet of insects of all stages, spiders and berries and seeds.

Nest A tight cup of weed stems, grasses, bark strips bound with plant fibers and lined with hair and rootlets. Mainly in dense bushes.

5¼ in

Considered to be the most gaudily colored North American bird, the painted bunting has a pleasing, vireo-like warbling song. Although a common garden bird within its range, it is difficult to see because of its shyness. To encourage this species to venture into gardens, a considerable amount of low, dense vegetation is required.

RUFOUS-SIDED TOWHEE *Pipilo erythrophthalmus*

THIS SPECIES CAN BE FOUND practically throughout the United States except for Oklahoma and Texas. In the southern half of the United States from Pennsylvania south, the population is permanent. In the west the population from Oregon and Washington south through the Great Basin is also permanent.

This is a large long-tailed un-sparrow like sparrow. The male has black hood and upperparts with rufous sides and white underparts. The black of the upperparts can show heavy spotting in western regions. Indeed, one form in the west was termed spotted towhee and had full species status for a long time. The female is brown where the male is black. Young birds are the most sparrow-like, showing heavy streaking on the back and underparts. The song is a familiar sound throughout the range and is easy to interpret as, *drink-your-tea*. They also give a *chew-whee* note. The towhee double rakes with its feet to expose seeds.

A common bird of a widespread group of habitats, in the east they frequent second growth areas, thickets and woodlands with underbrush. Where a suitable habitat is available they occur in city parks, backyards and gardens. In the west desert scrub, fence lines with thickets, brushy hill sides and even chaparral provide cover. Mainly a ground nester, the bulky cup of vine fiber, grasses and leaves can be placed above ground in dense bushes and even thick brushpiles. A hardy species, they are rapidly expanding their range northward.

Their presence is most often noticed as they scratch about under cover, tossing the leaves back with a quick

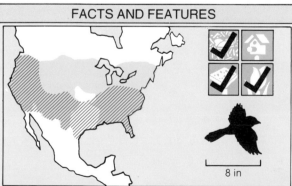

FACTS AND FEATURES

8 in

Plumage Male: black above with black hood. Western birds with white spotting on back. Rusty sides. White in outer tail tips. Female: brown where male is black.
Habitat Brushy fields, thickets, open forests with shrubby undercover, weedy hillsides, chaparral, parks.

Food Seeds, fruits of various sorts and wide variety of forest floor insects.
Nest Leaves, bark strips and twigs, lined with fine grasses or pine needles and tucked into a depression on the ground under cover of shrubs.

A common bird of city parks and gardens over much of the region, the towhee is slowly extending its range northward. It spends much of its time noisily raking through dead leaves under bushes for food. Nests are placed low down in a bush or on the ground.

kick of both feet at the same time—one of a few birds to do such a maneuver. Though they come out into open areas to feed, they require cover nearby. Brush piles are a real favorite, for not only will they provide protection from predation but they may also attract them as nesters. Densly planted areas of low canopy forms, such as juniper is also favored. They come to feeding areas and will feed on the ground or up on a feeding tray. A wide variety of seeds will be taken including sunflower seed, millet, fine cracked corn, and peanut kernels. Spreading the seed over a large area will encourage more birds to feed as this allows for feeding territory space. Collecting drying pigweed and amaranth and shaking it over the feeding site will allow for finer seed forms which are readily taken by this species.

127

BROWN TOWHEE *Pipilo fuscus*

A PERMANENT, COMMON RESIDENT throughout its range, this is a bird of the southwest and is found in extreme west Texas through New Mexico and Arizona and into south Colorado. A Pacific population is found from south Oregon through coastal California.

The Pacific race is brown backed with paler brown underparts and black streaking on the throat and upper breast. These stripes fuse into a black stick-pin spot on the chest. The interior form is brown capped and gray bodied. They have a singular black chest spot. Both groups have buffy undertail coverts. There is a great deal of variation in plumage color densities in this species.

As they scratch about with the two foot shuffling action of the towhee group, they often hold their tail cocked at a sharp angle and flick the tail by a rapid opening and closing motion. The call is a metallic *chip-chip-chip* for Pacific birds whereas the interior group has a distinct two note syllable often interpreted as *chili-chili-chili-chili-chili, chew-chew*

Again a distinct habitat preference can be seen for these two birds. The coastal group is definitely a backyard or garden park bird. It is also found in woodland edge and chaparral scrub whereas interior birds are of hill and mountain side scrub and rocky outcrops with grass and shrub cover. They are often seen as they fly from one place to another crossing openings or roads with rapid, loose wingbeats and then gliding.

The nest is rather bulky, loosely made of sticks and grasses tucked into a dense shrub. The first brood usually stays around the nest site well into the hatching of the next brood, still begging for food. At times it is the second hatching of birds that chases off the first chicks.

Dense undercover is a prime requirement for this species. Brush piles are key attractions, large bulky ones being the best. Water in a bath or lined depression is a sure attraction. A multitude of grasses are taken and if a weed patch is made available with wild oats, barley, rye and fescue grasses these birds will spend considerable time in such a plot. At the feeder, oats, millets, prosos, fine cracked corn and sunflower seeds are all taken. Often a family group will take up residence in an area and spend the entire year. The coastal race is particularly sedentary, and once established remains permanent.

FACTS AND FEATURES

8½ in

Plumage Brown or gray-brown above and lighter below. Buff throat may be bordered by streaks. Rusty undertail coverts and long tail.
Habitat Open brushy areas, weedy hillsides, chaparral, brushy riverine areas, gardens, cultivated land.
Food Seeds, fruits of many sorts, wide variety of insects.

Nest Deep cup of grasses and plant stems and bark strips. This is placed in a dense thicket, or hedgerow, quite often close to the ground.

The male and female of this species are similar. The necklace of spots bordering the throat and upper breast are distinctive. Juveniles are streaked, especially on the underparts, and all have rusty red vents. It can be distinguished from the green-tailed towhee by its plain brown back and tail.

SAVANNAH SPARROW *Passerculus sandwichensis*

This is a bird of open grassland. Various forms occur — a large pale form was formerly thought to be a separate species, the Ipswich sparrow. The heavily streaked underparts, yellowish line over eye, lack of black spot on the breast and short notched tail help to identify it.

A VERY WIDESPREAD SPECIES this bird breeds from Alaska south throughout Canada into the northeast United States south to Pennsylvania. It also breeds around the Great Lakes region and on west across Colorado to south California. It winters south of this area from the Carolinas across to mid-Texas and south. Many stay north of this line especially in the west coast area.

A short tailed, heavily streaked small sparrow, its tail has a decided fork to it. The legs are pale flesh colored. The head has a distinct cheek patch offset by eye lines which are rich yellow to the forepart. A pale central stripe runs down the center of the crown. Black malar marks are shown at the edge of the throat. Over their extensive range there is considerable color and size variation. The large northeast coastal form, known as the Ipswich sparrow is extremely pale and the west coast race is chocolate brown in marking. The song is a long, buzzy trill. The call is a distinct *tsit* note that once learned allows you to realize how common this species can be in a weedy area.

As you can imagine with such an extensive range, a wide variety of habitats is chosen, from the open high tundra to rolling grasslands and farmlands. Grassy coastland dunes are as favored as marsh edges and weedy fields. Seventeen recognized races occur, and any suitable habitat in the area might attract this species. The nest, made of grass, is tucked in the base of a grass clump with overhanging vegetation masking it.

Though not often seen at a feeding station, winter birds will come during harsh weather and feed on a variety of seeds. Allowing an area such as a garden or ploughed area to go to seed for the fall is a certain attraction. Here, pigweed, mugwort, and amaranths supply the bulk of their food. Brush piles located at the edges of open grassy areas are often a location for hiding or early morning singing or preening in the direct sun.

FACTS AND FEATURES

up to 6½ in

Plumage Highly variable but basically light brownish with heavy streaking below. Short tail, yellow at base of bill, pinkish legs and pale crown stripe.

Habitat From open tundra, coastal grasslands, prairies, marshes, farmland parks, beaches.

Food Mainly grass and weed seeds along with insects. Ipswich form will take aquatic larvae on beaches.

Nest A slight cup lining a depression in ground, sand, beneath grass tussock or tucked into tundra moss.

FIELD SPARROW *Spizella pusilla*

BASICALLY, THIS SPECIES IS FOUND IN the eastern half of the lower 48 states. It is pretty much a permanent resident throughout its range except for the northern edge in Maine and around the northern Great Lakes and the high prairie of the Dakotas. In mild winters many remain behind in this fringe region. There is a slight southern extension during the winter of some migrants to include southern Texas and mid-way down Florida.

A sleek, small sparrow of soft hues, its cap is pale rusty orange, the cheeks gray and the eye has a prominent white eye ring. The back is rusty with a white wing bar. The underparts are a grayish white to a buff color in some individuals. Notable is the pure pink bill.

These gregarious little sparrow travels about in small flocks. They frequent the weedy fields, old abandoned orchards and farmlands now laying in disuse. This change in agricultural practice has significantly increased their population in the last 15 years. However, as such areas revert to primary woodland or are developed, pockets with normally dense populations are dwindling. Outside of this, farmland and pinewoods with scrubby undergrowth are often favored. Unobtrusive in its ways, it often comes into city parks and gardens as long as weedy sites are available. The nest is a small cup of grasses and leaves lined with rootlets or animal hair which is placed on or within a foot of the ground. Starting nesting early in the spring usually allows the pair to produce three broods a year, especially in the south.

This is another species where brush piles, weedy fields and garden plots allowed to go to seed. Bristlegrass, panicgrass, crabgrass and dropseeds are high on the list of favorites. You can simply allow a plot to revert to a weed state or sow in mixed grasses. They will visit the winter feeding area and even come up to window ledges. There, peanut hearts, millets, and oil-seed sunflower are taken. They also relish thistle seed scattered about. In the spring, onion bags filled with animal fur (dog or horse hair) will be visited for nest lining. Be sure such a bag is placed near a limb so that the bird can pluck without hovering to reach.

FACTS AND FEATURES

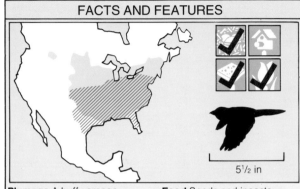

5½ in

Plumage A buffy orange brown with pale pink bill. Small head has a reddish crown and gray eye line. Very trim body.
Habitat Brushy clearing, farmland, secondary growth fields, powerlines, gardens, parkland.

Food Seeds and insects during the summer and mainly seeds and berries in winter.
Nest Tucked in a low bush. A cup of grasses, stems and rootlets with fine grass or hair lining.

The sexes are similar, and the most obvious distinguishing characteristic is the bright pink bill. Otherwise, rusty upperparts, unstreaked head, plain rump and double white wing bars help to identify it. The song begins with one or two clear, sweet whistles speeding up to a slurred warble.

FOX SPARROW *Passerella iliaca*

NESTING OCCURS THROUGHOUT Alaska on into northern Canada and it extends south into the mountains of the western United States and on the west coast. Wintering populations remain on the lower west coast and spread along a southern belt from Arizona and New Mexico east through central Texas and most of the southern states and Atlantic seaboard from extreme southern New England south.

This large, handsome sparrow is one of the most variable in color patterns. Subspecies range in color from foxy reds, that give the species its name, to grays and dark brown. In general it is a stocky bird, reddish brown to grayish brown above with heavy markings on the underparts merging into a spot on the upper breast. The bill is large and conical. The song is loud and sweet but is usually only heard on the breeding grounds of the far north.

This is a bird that most people are familiar with as it visits the feeding station scratching about with its double-leg kick method. It will scrape about in the thickets and underbrush and may be overlooked, until you are attracted by the sound of the scratching. In the far north it lives in the shrubby willows of open tundra pockets and south of that area coastal thickets, brushy hillsides and the chaparral covered slopes. During migration it is to be expected in any type of brushy habitat. Parklands, weedy fields, gardens with dense cover even city parks will attract their share. The numbers vary: some years produce a huge population and others only a few birds.

The nest is a large affair built on or close to the ground in a dense thicket in coniferous woods or shrubs of open tundra. In the far north caribou or moose hair is used as a nest lining.

At the bird tray during the winter they are most attracted to sunflower seeds, but peanut kernels, fine cracked corn and millets will also be taken. Be sure water is made available and that a thick cover of evergreen or brush pile is nearby for cover. Thickets and weed fields will often hold a population for a considerable time and will be an alternative to the feeding station.

FACTS AND FEATURES

7 in

Plumage Quite variable. From rich foxy red to grays. All have heavy marked underparts with triangular spots. Rust rump in most.
Habitat Scrub woodlands on mountain nesting areas, brushy hillsides, weed fields, thickets in parks and gardens.

Food While nesting, mainly insects. Other times: seeds and fruits of a wide variety. Sunflower, millet, fine cracked corn.
Nest Large cup in dense brush of grass, rootlets and leaves. Often lined with hair or feathers.

A large sparrow with highly variable plumage patterns, coloration and bill size, ranging from deep chocolate brown upperparts to reddish brown and gray brown. Most forms, however, have a reddish rump and tail. Underparts are always heavily streaked with a large, dark central spot on the breast.

TREE SPARROW *Spizella arborea*

This is the largest of the sparrows with a rufous cap. The sexes are similar. The plain grayish underparts with a dark central spot on the breast immediately identify it. Two bold white wing bars, notched tail and dark legs are other useful features. The song begins with one or two high notes followed by a rapid warble.

THE BREEDING RANGE of this species is through mid-Alaska across the high arctic of Canada to a southern limit of south Hudson Bay and on the west coast into British Columbia. Wintering populations stretch from coast to coast in the contiguous 48 states, from Washington to the Great Lakes on through New England and south to the Carolinas, north Texas and north California.

This striking sparrow is easy to identify with its rufous cap, clear gray underparts with black "stickpin" chest spot and chestnut patches to the side of the breast. The back is orange chestnut streaked with white and black. Note the yellow color of the lower mandible.

Once it leaves its northern nesting territory, the first arrivals are seen at the wintering grounds in early fall. They remain through the winter and depart with the first signs of spring. It is only in the spring that the sweet, rich notes of its song are heard before its departure north. It prefers brushy areas, weed fields, and open areas including the marshlands of the coast. It is very gregarious during the winter and large flocks often roost together in deep grass areas or dense brush piles.

This is certainly one of the main winter visitors to the feeding station. It will take a wide variety of foods, from peanut butter imbeded with bird seed to millets, peanut kernels, and oil-seed sunflower as well as black-striped sunflower. Ample cover is needed near the feeding station as well as a dense brush pile for night roosting. Low shrubby junipers, yews and cedars provide excellent cover as well as night shelter during storms.

FACTS AND FEATURES

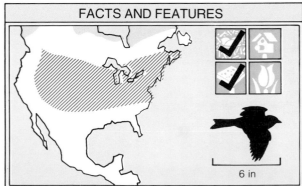

6 in

Plumage Rufous cap; gray head; yellow lower mandible; chestnut back; gray underparts with black chest spot.
Habitat Breeds in the extreme northern arctic zones. In winter favors thickets, brushy areas, farmlands, feeding stations.

Food On breeding grounds, mainly insects and some seeds. In winter areas seeds are taken.
Nest Bulky cup of grasses and sedges. Often lined with caribou hair in arctic.

CHIPPING SPARROW *Spizella passerina*

A VERY WIDE-SPREAD SPECIES, the chipping sparrow ranges from the Alaska panhandle, throughout Canada and throughout the 48 states except for the high area of the Texas panhandle and Oklahoma. Florida and southern Texas are only visited during the winter.

This familiar species is easy to recognize in adult plumage. The brick red cap contrasts to the gray white line over the eye. A black line runs from the base of the bill through the eye to the nape. The bill is small and black. The neck, cheeks and underparts are gray without any markings. The back is black lined with brown, and the rump is gray. Young birds and fall birds have brownish cheeks, thin streaked crown and gray rumps. The tail is deeply forked.

The "chippie" is one of the most familiar of all the sparrows located in the backyard or evergreen next to the house. Often seen on the ground collecting nesting material or feeding on grass seeds, they appear to shuttle about sitting very tight to the ground. Weed fields, scrubby areas, old orchards, lawns, wood edges, parks and gardens are but a few of the wide diversity of habitat chosen by this species. The staccato prolonged call is truly a sound of spring and early summer as they call from building tops, evergreens or powerlines. They often will allow a very close approach before flying off. A conifer is the preferred nesting site but shrubs will also be chosen. A well made cup of grasses and plant fibers is often lined with animal fur or fine rootlets. Two clutches are normal. In the fall, flocks of these birds move to feed in open wooded glades and lawns before shifting to the southern part of their range for wintering.

This is not the type of bird you can directly attract with feeding stations or plantings. Because of their ability to live near humans they are a normal part of the backyard bird population. However, planting trees such as blue spruce, yew, arborvitae, and other dense evergreens increase the chances of having a nesting pair. Lawns and open areas will provide food. Birdbaths will be frequented and brush piles are enjoyed for cover and fall get-togethers. During the winter they will come to feeding areas under stressed conditions and millet, peanut hearts and oil-seed are taken.

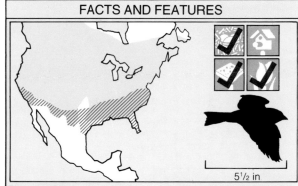

FACTS AND FEATURES

5½ in

Plumage Sleek sparrow with chestnut crown, black eye line and white stripe over eye. Small bill. Gray below and chestnut brown on back.
Habitat Open areas of all types. Lawns, parks, orchards, backyards, farmlands, prairie etc.

Food Smaller seeds of grass and weeds, insects, spiders and other invertebrates.
Nest A tightly woven cup of grasses often in an ornamental shrub near a house. Likes evergreens. Nest lined with animal hair.

In summer, the rufous cap, white eye stripe over a black line through eye, plain gray breast and all black bill separate the chipping from all other sparrows. Immatures and adults in winter can be distinguished by a gray rump contrasting with a brown back. The song is a dry, flat trill of chip notes.

SONG SPARROW *Melospiza melodia*

THIS SPECIES IS FOUND from the Aleutian chain through Alaska and Canada south to Mexico on the west coast, New Mexico, Kansas, Arkansas and South Carolina. Wintering birds can be found throughout the United States from the southern tip of Alaska south.

There is a great disparity in sizes in this species. Birds in the Aleutians being very large and dark compared to the small light colored birds of the southwestern extremes. Basically it is a long tailed sparrow with heavy streaking on the underparts fusing into a dark chest spot, with two additional throat spots caused by the increased size of the malar stripe. The face is grayish with a gray stripe over the eye and down the center of the brown cap. The song is also varied on a local dialect basis with more than 13 distinct variations. In most cases it is introduced by a series of three *seet, seet, seet* notes followed by a bubbling trill.

One of the commonest birds in the United States, they are a permanent resident in most areas frequented. They are birds of thickets, hedgerows, brush piles, fields and pond margins, not only in suburban and country situations but within city parks, abandoned lots and gardens. The cup nest made mainly of woven grasses is placed on the ground or in dense scrub bases up to four feet off the ground. In mid-summer the male may be seen solely caring for the young as the female incubates the next clutch of eggs.

During breeding season, weedy areas and brush piles are the greatest attractants. Here the nest may be placed, or the areas used for feeding or sitting in the morning sun and singing. Cover in feeding areas is a prerequisite for regular visits. During the winter when they come to feed on seed scattered on the ground or up to a low feeding shelf, escape shrubs or brush piles should be in easy reach. Smaller seeds are favored such as the white and red proso millet. In recent years, oil-seed sunflower has been a desired food. Water should be made available during nesting and the winter months. If there are weed patches (with pigweed and amaranth) flocks passing through from the north can reach substantial numbers in the fall.

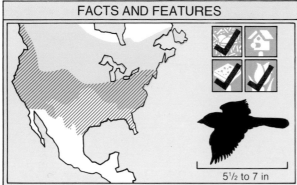

FACTS AND FEATURES

5½ to 7 in

Plumage Another variable species. Dark stripes bordering a white throat, and streaking of upper breast coalese into a dark central spot. Long tailed.
Habitat Swampy thickets, dry thickets, brushy areas, hedgerows, gardens, farmlands, any open weedy area.

Food Mainly grass and weed seeds, but insects and invertebrates are also taken.
Nest On the ground or in dense low bush. Cup of grasses and rootlets with finer grass lining.

One of the commonest of the sparrows, much admired for its song. It is highly variable in size and coloration but the long-tailed pumping action in flight and distinct chimp *call note are diagnostic. Note also the heavily streaked breast with its central spot.*

WHITE-THROATED SPARROW *Zonotrichia albicollis*

BREEDING FROM THE YUKON east in Canada, this species extends into New England south to Connecticut and over into Pennsylvania. Also around the northern Great Lakes Region. In the winter, the white-throated sparrow can be found from southern Vermont, New Hampshire and mid-New York, south to northern Florida, eastern Kansas and to the Rio Grande Valley in Texas. A splinter population winters on the southern California coast into extreme southern Arizona and New Mexico.

The sparrow is a very large, handsome bird with a striking black and white striped head and pure white throat. The lores (area between eye and bill) is a rich yellow. The underparts are gray and the back, brown streaked with tan and black. Young birds in the fall have gray throats and dusky head markings, and lack the yellow lores. The crown striping is usually tan.

They breed in deep coniferous forests or bog areas. The nest, a cup of grasses, is placed on the ground often tucked in under vegetation. In migration and on wintering grounds, they are found in dense brush, thick undergrowth, swampy areas, hedgerows and weed fields. Usually, you are first aware of their presence when you hear the scratching of leaves. They scratch about with both feet at the same time. Slow in their movements, they are not quick to fly off when discovered. They respond very well to "squeaking" and will often hop into sight to check out the intruder. The loud, ringing, *oh sweet, sweet, sweet* is one of the pure sounds of the northwoods.

As one of the "sure-fire" feeder group. They come readily to a winter feeding station and will usually spend the entire winter if brush piles and dense conifers are available for roosting and protection. They are highly gregarious and move about in flocks of possibly related clans. The first order of preference at the feeder is sunflower seed. Striped or oil-seed, millet, peanut kernels, fine cracked corn and scattered thistle seed are also taken. They seem to enjoy having water available and will bathe even in the coldest weather. Reluctant to go too high to a feeding tray, ground feeders are best.

FACTS AND FEATURES

Plumage Alternating white and black stripes on crown. Yellow spot between eye and bill. Distinctive white throat. Grayish white below, striped brown back.

Habitat Edges of coniferous woods, in bogs and wet grassy areas. Weed fields, brushy hillsides and swampy areas. Parks.

Food Weed seeds of many varieties, insects. At feeders loves oil-seed and sunflower.

Nest A cup of fine grasses, rootlets, and other plant fibers. Built at base of grass clump or moss hummock.

7 in

This is a large sparrow similar in appearance to the white-crowned, but with a shorter neck, white throat, dark bill and the yellow spot between eye and bill to separate it. The call note is a lisping tseet. It usually feeds on the ground.

WHITE-CROWNED SPARROW *Zonotrichia leucophrys*

The white-crowned is distinguished from the similar white-throated sparrow by its pinkish or yellowish bill, ill defined dusky white throat patch and lack of yellow spot between bill and eye. The variable song usually consists of clear whistles followed by a faster descending trill.

THIS IS A COMMON NESTING species from Alaska throughout the Canadian sub-arctic to Labrador. In the west the range extends south to central California, Nevada and central Arizona. A wintering population can be found in a narrow coastal strip from the southern tip of Alaska to the Mexican border. The remainder of wintering birds are found south of a line running from Wyoming through Missouri to Maryland.

The adult bird is striking with its crisp black and white head pattern. The face and neck is a deep gray and blends into the chest and upper belly. The flanks are buffy and the back a streaked brown and chestnut. The immature birds have a pale bill, lack the black and white crown but have rusty stripes in their place. They are long tailed, gray rumped, large sparrows.

On the nesting grounds, it is a bird of the open tundra and scrub bog, and shrubby habitat such as willow thickets. In the winter they show up in many environments, out in the open on grassy areas, in weedy fields and thickets. They are well adapted to living with people and will nest right next to the house in suitable habitat. The nest is a grass cup well hidden in overhanging vegetation.

Weed fields, garden plots gone to seed and any garden may attract this species as a migrant or winter resident. They come readily to feeding stations. Here they enjoy water all year-round and many seed types are taken. Oilseed sunflower is the favorite but striped sunflower is

taken with about as much rapidity. Both white and red proso millet are on the favored list. Large, loose brush piles are preferred as nesting and roosting sites and communal meeting places. In parks they will quickly become tame and take bread and other items from peoples' hands.

FACTS AND FEATURES

Plumage Bright black and white striped crown positioned to the forward angle of the head. Gray body with brown back. A large sparrow. Young with rusty cap line.
Habitat Open woodlands, tundra, weedy fields, parks, coastal scrub. Comes to feeders in winter.

Food Insects and berries. Seeds in winter.
Nest Sheltered by grass or moss clump on ground. Cup of grasses; rootlets and hair lined.

up to 7 in

DARK-EYED JUNCO *Junco hyemalis*

AT SOME TIME OF THE YEAR one form or another of this species is found throughout North America except for the high arctic. Breeding ranges extend from Alaska through Canada and into the Northeast, Great Lakes region and mountain areas of the west and far west coast. Wintering populations shift south a bit and many winter on the Mexican border and south tip of Florida.

This species shows a number of variations and there are at least five well marked subspecies. They all have pink bills and white outer tail feathers along with white underparts and, as the name implies, dark eyes. The slate colored form is all slate above and onto the chest. The Oregon form has a dark hood that contrasts to the rich brown back and white of the belly. Gray-headed forms are basically all gray with a small rusty area on the back and deep black smudging near the eye. All other intermediates are along these lines. The basic song pattern is a prolonged monotonous trill.

These birds are ground foraging species that flick their tails while feeding or when they fly. The flash of white is a key feature for identification. They do not scratch about for food but rather pick about in a more deliberate search for insects, larvae, egg cases and seeds. As one might expect, with so many races all types of habitat are frequented. In general, however, conifer woodlands are the favored habitat or mixed conifer birch aspen groves. In such areas look for them in the glades or transition areas with brooks, or open "balds." Here they forage in the broken shadows. On wintering grounds brushy fields, weedy patches, gardens and brushy piles are favored.

Formerly split into several different species, this variably plumaged species is now recognized as one species with different forms. White outer tail feathers are common to all and are conspicuous in flight. The song is a slow, musical trill on one pitch.

♂

FACTS AND FEATURES

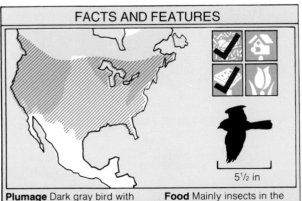

5½ in

Plumage Dark gray bird with white belly in east; brown bird with black hood in west; all gray bird with rusty back in southwest. All have white outer tail feathers.
Habitat Mixed woodlands, coniferous forest, forest edge, wooded hillsides, canyons etc.

Food Mainly insects in the summer and seeds in the winter. Eats springtails on snow fields.
Nest A cup of grasses, rootlets, bark strips and hair tucked into bank under rock overhang, in tree roots, etc.

They are one of the most familiar species at backyard feeding stations.

With the first signs of winter approaching the dark-eyed junco move in. Though they may move off and forage in nearby weedy areas during good weather, at the first sign of a storm a heavy feeding period will ensue. They enjoy a wide variety of seeds including millets, canary seed, thistle seed, fine cracked corn and oil-seed sunflower. Normally they prefer to feed directly on the ground but will come up to a ledge feeder. A nearby cover is needed for escape and dense conifers for night roosts.

137

DICKCISSEL *Spiza americana*

THE DICKCISSEL IS A RATHER unique finch of the midwestern prairies, ranging from Montana to the Great Lakes region then south through Texas with the bulk of the population on the eastern edge of this region. Though wintering in Mexico and northern South America a substantial number of birds show up in the east and west at winter feeding stations. In general the range is expanding eastward with populations being re-established in classic areas of the past, to as far east as Washington D.C.

In body shape and actions they are very similar to the house sparrow *(passer domesticus)*. The female birds and immatures have a similar plumage to the female house sparrow. However, there is usually a yellowish tint to the breast and the broad malar stripes help separate them when mixed in with a milling flock of sparrows at the feeder. The male is quite handsome, with rich yellow belly offset by a black bib. The wings show a bright rusty shoulder patch. The call is a distinct *dick ciss ciss ciss*.

Across the grasslands of the mid-west this species appears to be on every fence and powerline exclaiming its territory. Open weedy area, farmlands, pasture lots, feeding pens and grainfields, all of these attract large numbers of birds. They are highly gregarious throughout most of the year and in southern areas, during migration, incredible flocks of hundreds may be encountered. Although some areas report shrinking numbers, in general the population seems quite healthy.

Outside the central band of nesting, this species is often seen for the first time at the winter feeding site. Though they will on occasion come up to feed at a tray, they prefer to feed directly on seeds cast on the ground. Sunflower, millet, and fine cracked corn belie their background as "grain belt" species, and are the selected items. Weedy garden plots left to seed are also a major attraction and they will join in with the sparrows and other species to forage for food in such sites. Brush piles nearby are ideal for overnight shelter and protection from predators.

FACTS AND FEATURES

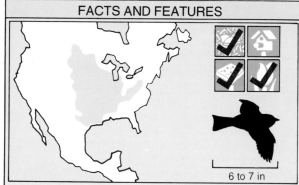

6 to 7 in

Plumage Male: bright yellow chest with black crescent. Gray head, brown back, bright chestnut shoulder patch. Female: brownish, darker on back with yellow tint to breast.
Food Grass seeds, grains, insects. At feeder, oil-seed sunflower and fine cracked corn.

Nest A cup of grasses and rootlets built on the ground or close to it in dense shrubbery.

Breeding mainly in the Prairie States, the male suggests a small meadowlark when in breeding dress, while the female recalls a female house sparrow, but its clearer eye stripe and yellow tinge on the breast will separate it.

EASTERN MEADOWLARK *Sturnella magna*

THE RANGE OF THE EASTERN BIRD is throughout the east from Maine to Florida and west to south Arizona and New Mexico north through Oklahoma, Nebraska and central Minnesota. It is a permanent resident in that range except for the high plains and extreme northern areas. The range overlap with the western meadowlark occurs on the great plains and in the southwestern sector.

Although the eastern and western meadowlark are a classic case of two species with overlapping ranges and almost identical in pattern they do not interbreed and are therefore full species.

This species is strictly a bird of the grasslands and it is easy to see the various physical adaptations for this life. Long legs, camouflaged back, yet with bright yellow underparts sporting a large black V across the chest. This acts as a flash signal when presented from atop a grass clump. The bird can go from the dull browns of the back pattern to the brilliant underparts quickly, acting very similar to semiphore. The outer tail feathers are white and flash when the bird takes flight. The bill is long and the eyes placed at the base so the bird can simply wedge the bill under an object, open the bill and peer directly under the object to see if a food morsel is present.

It is found in the open grasslands, prairies, farmlots and saltmarsh grasslands of its range. The mellow high pitched whistle given from a grass tussock or tree at meadow edge, is a familiar country and plains sound.

The nest is a grass cup placed on the ground and arched over with plant material. The birds do not fly directly to the nest but land a distance away and walk to the site.

Though they live in grain areas, very little grain is taken. Rather the abundant insect population is fed on, with some grain supplementing the diet during harsh winter months.

If fields or open grassy areas are nearby the possibility of seeing and hearing this species is high. They do not come to feeders even in the harshest conditions. Orchards may be visited during the winter where apples supplement the diet.

The meadowlark is more likely to be encountered in open prairie country, especially the grain areas. It feeds mainly on insects. However, grain is taken in the winter months when it will also take fallen fruit.

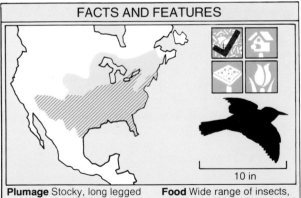

FACTS AND FEATURES

10 in

Plumage Stocky, long legged grassland bird. Brown back, chest a brilliant yellow with large black V. Outer tail feathers white.
Habitat Grasslands, prairies, grainfields, farmland, coastal marsh grasslands.

Food Wide range of insects, grubs, grass seeds and weed seeds. In marsh areas also takes young snails.
Nest A cup of grasses tucked into a depression in field under grass clump.

139

BROWN-HEADED COWBIRD *Molothrus ater*

FOUND THROUGHOUT THE LOWER 48 states of the United States, this bird is a permanent resident in the eastern half and southern part of its range. In the northwest and Canada the population is a summering one but the line of permanency appears to be slowly moving northward.

The male is easy to distinguish with its copper colored head and bright metallic blue black body. The female is a drab brownish gray with faint breast streaking. The young birds are similar to the female but are heavily streaked and are often mistaken for a sparrow. Blackbirds walk about and sparrows do not, so that habit alone separates the major grouping.

Highly gregarious, they spend most of the year mixed in with other blackbirds wandering farmlands, open countrysides, prairies, cattle yards and meadows. They come into the city and appear en masse on lawns, in parks, backyards, orchards and coastal marshes.

This is the only true nest parasite in North America. They build no nest whatsoever, depositing their eggs in the nests of others. Supposedly this habit began as an efficient way to stay with the food supply, stirred up by the migrant buffalo herds. With this random wandering, staying in one place to raise young was out of the question. A wide variety of hosts are known but several seem to be favored victims. Phoebes, yellow warblers, red-eyed vireos, song and chipping sparrows top the list. The birds have also been shown to play a vital role in reducing the population of the endangered Kirtland's warbler and measures had to be taken to reduce this parasitism.

Once they have deposited their eggs they feed on insects, grubs, fruits and berries and some seeds. The fall sees massive build-ups of the species. What is interesting is that the birds raised by "foster parents" do not imprint on that species but reunite with pure cowbird flocks after the nesting season. A rather unique trait but one that points out the distinct evolution of parasitism. At this time the backyard feeder becomes one of their points of focus and flocks visit daily. They enjoy breadcrumbs, fine cracked corn and sunflower seeds. All other seeds are taken when the favorites are depleted. Their presence often brings in other blackbirds and the feeding tray may be monopolized by this mixed flock. Though they do fly up to feeders, they prefer ground feeding and in that way other birds can get to feed.

FACTS AND FEATURES

7 in

Plumage Male: coppery brown hood contrasting to metallic blue purple of body. Female: grayish brown.
Habitat Open areas, prairies, woodland edges, farmlands, parks, gardens.
Food Grain, seeds, berries and other fruit. Some insects and invertebrates.

Nest None: always parasitizes other species: favors phoebe, yellow warbler, song sparrow and red-eyed vireo.

A summer visitor to the more northerly parts of its range, the brown-headed cowbird is becoming more of a resident in these areas. Males are easily identified by the combination of black body and brown head. Females and young are best told by the finch-like, conical bill.

♂

BREWER'S BLACKBIRD *Euphagus cyanocephalus*

♂

Brewer's blackbird resembles a short-tailed grackle, with highly iridescent plumage reflecting green and purple in strong light. At a distance, however, it appears black. Females are brownish-gray with dark eyes, which helps to separate it from the rusty blackbird.

ONE OF THE MOST COMMON birds of the west coast, the summer population extends east into Canada and as far as the Great Lakes and south to Nebraska. The permanent western population reaches as far east as Colorado. During the winter the population shifts to a band running from Arizona east through Oklahoma and on into the Carolinas, south into the southern tip of Florida and the Mexican border of Texas. Within this wintering area huge flocks build up and dark masses can often be seen covering agricultural areas.

Their plumage is an iridescent black with the head area appearing purplish. The eye is a bright yellow. The tail is short and rounded and their walking manner is typical of the blackbird sub-family.

A wide variety of habitats are visited. Sites include farmland, cattle range, meadows, parkland, lakeshores and coastal plains.

They forage for food in large flocks which increases their success in finding insects, larval forms, seeds and fruits. A wide variety of invertebrates make up the bulk of their diet. They visit crop areas and rangelands mainly after the harvest period when they can clean up the remaining grain.

The nest is a well made cup consisting of grasses, twigs, and rootlets. The inside is made of mud or cow manure and then lined with additional grasses and rootlets. Though nests have been found on the ground in fields, they are usually placed in dense shrubs or trees. Being a gregarious species they often nest in loose colonies and go off to forage for food together.

Winter populations will come into feeding stations. They favor feeding directly on the ground. All forms of seeds are taken from fine cracked corn, sunflower seeds, millet, to peanut hearts and even peanut butter with suet and seeds made into cakes and set out in tins. If weedy fields or agricultural land are nearby they are sure to visit at some point and this often leads to them investigating backyard feeding stations.

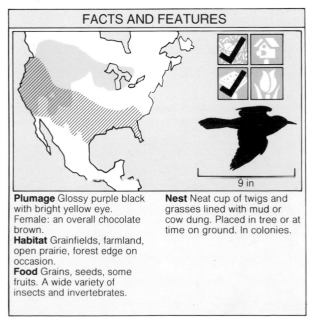

FACTS AND FEATURES

Plumage Glossy purple black with bright yellow eye. Female: an overall chocolate brown.
Habitat Grainfields, farmland, open prairie, forest edge on occasion.
Food Grains, seeds, some fruits. A wide variety of insects and invertebrates.

Nest Neat cup of twigs and grasses lined with mud or cow dung. Placed in tree or at time on ground. In colonies.

9 in

RED-WINGED BLACKBIRD *Agelaius phoeniceus*

THIS IS ONE OF THE BEST known birds and certainly one of the commonest in North America, the range even extending into southern Alaska. Found in every state, it remains a permanent resident in all but the extreme north of its territory. During the winter enormous flocks build up in the southern section. Some of these flocks have been estimated to be in excess of 11 million birds. There is a distinct spring movement and for many the loud *ok-a-lee* given from tree top or cattail stub, signals spring.

The male, garbed in deep black and with brilliant shoulder patches edged below with yellow, is unmistakable. The female, however, looks more like a large sparrow, brown in color with buffy underparts and heavily streaked with markings above and below. Some females may show a red tinge to the shoulder. Also, many have an almost orange throat. In migration the males always arrive first, set up a territory and in a few weeks the females arrive.

They have a wide variety of habitat preference. Cattail marshes are the ideal. Upland meadows are used and farmfields, woodland edges, and swamplands. They often feed in grainfields and non-wet areas. They come into backyards, especially in migration and in winter and often the yard explodes with sounds as a flock pitches in for a visit.

The nest is woven with plant material from the area chosen. In marshes it is marsh vegetation, leaves, cattail and rootlets. In field situations it is almost purely grasses and sedges with some leaf material. The nest may be directly on the ground or in a shrub, cattail clump or similar vegetation. It is attached firmly by plant fibers to the crotch of stalks of the plants.

Groups of birds are quick to visit the backyard feeders in migration or wintering groups, and will often stay for long periods of time. A wide variety of seeds are taken. Finely cracked corn is a favorite as are sunflower seeds, but millets, sourgums, peanut hearts etc are all consumed. It should be noted that during the summer insects form the bulk of the diet and that grains are mainly consumed after the harvesting season. It has been shown that the insect consumption far outweighs any grain they injest and though considered as vermin by some, the birds on their breeding grounds are most beneficial.

This is one bird that at some point will visit any feeder, even in city backyard plots.

FACTS AND FEATURES

Plumage All glossy black with red shoulder patches bordered on bottom with yellow. Female: heavily streaked brown, may show tint of red in wing.
Habitat Cattail marshes, upland grassland, farmland, coastal marshes, wood edges, cultivated land.

Food Insects, invertebrates, wide range of seeds. Corn a favorite.
Nest A cup of grasses, plant fibers and bark strips. Placed in grass tussock, woven onto marsh vegetation or in crotch of scrub trees.

8¾ in

The male's red shoulder patches broadly edged with buffish yellow are not always easy to see when the bird is perched. The similar tricolored blackbird has white edges to the shoulder patches. Females are heavily streaked below and brown above.

COMMON GRACKLE *Quiscalus quiscula*

THIS COMMON SPECIES has a wide range in the contiguous 48 states extending into central and southeastern Canada. Permanent throughout most of the eastern portion, the western range of summering birds extends to western Montana, Colorado and New Mexico. The westward expansion of the range seems inevitable as more records are occurring each spring on the west coast.

For a long time this species was considered to be two and termed the purple grackle and bronze grackle based on the sheen of the feathers. This was finally proved to be no more than local color variation. Birds of the northeast and west of the Appalachian chain tend to be bronzed bodied with purple sheen head. Birds east of the Appalachians tend to be more iridescent purple. All birds show a very long tail that forms a large V shape when in good plumage. The eyes are pale yellow. Young or moulting grackles with short tails can be confused with Brewer's blackbird.

Like most of the blackbirds they are very gregarious and move about in very large flocks. Open fields, pastureland, cattle feed lots, grain fields and other agricultural land are all frequented. But they also can be seen foraging about in flocks on woodland floors, swamplands, marshes, parks and gardens. During migration flocks will often pour into a backyard and dominate the feeding tray.

The bulky stick nest is placed in a variety of locations but most often in an evergreen or dense forest edge tree. They nest in loose colonies when prime sites are available. However, individual birds have been found nesting in tree holes, in cliff face cavities, open buildings and even on the stick edge of an osprey nest. This high level of adaptability accounts for its success and abundance.

At the feeding tray these birds dominate all others. Often arriving in flocks, the feeding area is quickly depleted of its seeds, breadcrumbs and whatever items have been placed out. In the field a wide variety of food is taken, from insects, larvae, pupae, spiders, worms and other invertebrates to young birds and eggs found in ground nests or located in tree sites. Even small reptiles are taken. This voracity seems to reach its peak when food is difficult to obtain and they will attack other birds and rip into their crop once killed. Certainly not an ideal garden visitor to the feeding tray but one that is inevitable.

FACTS AND FEATURES

Plumage Long keel-shaped tail. Two color forms: bronze bodied with purple head. Overall purple sheen. Females a uniform brown.
Habitat Open woodlands, fields, farmlands, parks, gardens, lawns. Any open area where seeds and insects occur will attract flocks.

Food Insects, grass seeds, but a wide variety of other objects from worms to eggs and young birds.
Nest A bulky mass of twigs, leaves and debris. Often with mud lining and fine grasses.

12½ in

♂

Common grackles are often seen in flocks. The variable iridescent plumage, yellow eye, and long keel-shaped tail help identify the male. Females are smaller and duller. At long range or in poor light, males look all black. The call is a loud chuck *and the short, squeaky song is distinctive.*

BOAT-TAILED GRACKLE *Quiscalus major*

KNOWN AS A TRUELY COASTAL BIRD, this species extends from mid-New Jersey in a slim band along the Atlantic seaboard. Then throughout Florida but again remaining strictly coastal along the Gulf Coast states and on to the upper coast of Texas. Indications are that the population will continue to creep northward.

This very large blackbird is unmistakable. Its long keel shaped tail makes up nearly one half of the total bird's length. The glossy blue-black plumage blends into a glossy purple head. Within the range the eye color varies from yellow in the northern part to dark in Gulf Coast birds. The female is as handsome as the male. Though the tail is not as long or keel shaped it is large for any bird. The soft yellow tans of the underparts contrast to the darker back and wings.

Within its range coastal marshes are indeed favorite foraging areas. However, they also frequent grasslands, open woodland edges, grass prairies, feed lots, cattle pens and in city situations, parks, gardens, and even the smallest clumps of trees within the city. In the evening and early morning, these highly gregarious birds serenade from their tree roosts (palms being a favorite) with the loudest jumble of *squeaks*, *squacks*, and "electronic" sounds one could imagine. This chatter goes on well into the night and only subsides in the morning as massive flocks move off to feed in the surrounding area.

Colonies of birds nest together and the large bulky nests fill clumps of trees. The nest is a jumble of leaves, grasses, and debris found locally. It is lined with mud and then grasses are added for a final mat for the eggs. At these colonies during nest building and when raising the young, the sounds can be nearly deafening!

Within their range if groves of trees are present the species can take over. Though they may nest in your backyard or on your street it doesn't necessarily mean they will frequent your feeder. Quite often they are more content to fly off to the shore line or lake edge to forage. However, if they do visit, the seeds put out will disappear quickly. Cracked corn and sunflower seeds are favored.

Often they join with other migrant black birds in staggering flocks of thousands that form ribbons through the sky when they are returning to roost sites.

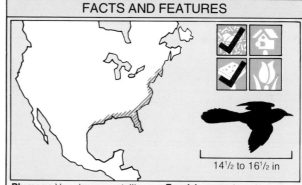

FACTS AND FEATURES

14½ to 16½ in

Plumage Very large, metallic purple blue bird with long tail that forms a V shape. Female is a tawny brown with darker wings and tail.
Habitat Coastal areas, wet meadows, riverine forests, farmland, parks. Often roosts in palms in south.

Food Appears to eat everything! Seeds, fruits, insects, small mammals, etc.
Nest A bulky mass in a tree usually near water. Made of grasses, twigs and plant stems. Mud interior lined with rootlets. In colonies.

♂

Related to the blackbirds and orioles, this species is the largest representative of this family in North America. In some parts of its range it is known as the "Jackdaw."

SCOTT'S ORIOLE *Icterus parisorum*

Strikingly colored black and yellow, the male is easily distinguished. Females and immatures, however, can be very confusing and care should be taken when attempting to identify them.

THIS IS A COMMON BIRD in the arid and semi-arid areas of the southwest. The boundaries of its range are confined to southern California, lower Nevada and Utah, throughout Arizona and most of New Mexico and the arid Big Bend country of Texas.

Passing through this area you are sure to encounter this rather large oriole, striking in its lemon yellow plumage with black hood extending onto the back and well down on the chest. The wings are black with a large yellow shoulder patch. The female is much more subdued, in light lemon color with dark wings and streaked back.

The species seem to have favored trees and they are very active chasing about within the groves. Palms, Joshua trees, yucca, and even pinyon pine are most often visited. More often than not a palm, such as Washingtonia, or a yucca is the chosen spot for nesting. The pendulant, beautifully woven structure is often hidden behind downward hanging limbs and is woven from long fibers pulled from the edges of the leaves.

Insects are chased about in the foliage but seeds are also taken. Flowers will be visited and the long bill probes deep for nectar as well as visiting insects.

The key to attracting this bird is twofold. Plantings of palm or yucca provides suitable nesting sites should a bird visit. Secondly, sugar water bottles may be placed out. Not only will these attract hummingbirds, but these orioles will visit them constantly to get the nectar-like water. A perch should be provided as the birds do not have the ability to hover. Additional food items include fruit, and oranges are a favorite. These can be wedged in a tree crotch or placed on a peg board. Although some seeds may be taken from a feeding tray, the fruit and "nectar" will be the main choice.

Ample cover should be provided for escape routes and, as with all desert and arid country species, water is a main attraction. Dripping water, or if possible water running into a pool will be selected over standing water. Cool desert oases often provide this setting. Yucca or palm for nesting, flowers and a stream trickling over the rocks is an excellent area to visit to see the type of arrangement you can establish to attract these birds.

FACTS AND FEATURES

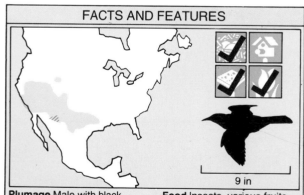

9 in

Plumage Male with black hood that extends onto the back and down the chest. Wings black with yellow shoulder. Tail black. Rest of body lemon yellow. Female without hood and duller wing and tail.
Habitat Semi arid areas with yuccas, palms and oak/pinyon forest.

Food Insects, various fruits and flower nectar. Will come to sugar water bottles.
Nest Pendant nest of grasses and plant fibers woven to the hanging leaf of a palm or yucca.

NORTHERN ORIOLE *Icterus galbula*

DUE TO RECENT RE-CLASSIFICATION the range of this species is coast to coast (including central southern Canada) and it is a summer resident in every state except Florida!

In the past we had two species to deal with. The Bullock's oriole of the west, and the Baltimore of the east. Studies in the mid-west in areas of overlap showed that the species were freely interbreeding and that the hybrid showed traits of both. However, we can still recognize pure forms in the distant regions and often a skewing to one race or the other with the hybrids.

The "Baltimore" type is deep orange with a totally black hood running down onto the back and well down the breast. The wings are black with orange shoulders, and the tail black in the center and orange to the outside. The Bullock race is black and orange also. However, the

Colored orange and black, the male is unmistakable. Females and young, however, may be confused with other species, but the breast is more yellow-orange. It may be separated from all female tanagers by bill shape, and from all but the western tanager by its two wing bars.

black on the head is confined to the crown and a black line through the eye. The back is black as are the wings but the shoulder area sports bright white patches. The throat is black and the remainder of the underparts orange. Like its eastern form the tail is black and orange. The female of the Baltimore is distinctly orange whereas the female Bullock's is a lemon yellow with gray white underbelly.

Both species are birds of open woodlands, farmfield edges, parklands, gardens and shade trees lining the streets in the city. A favored habitat is riverine forest and it is in such a habitat that the populations meet and interbreed on the great plains.

The nest is perhaps one of the best known of all birds. A long pendulant structure of grass and plant fibers that is covered with plant down, and spider web, with fibers from milkweed being a common "suturing" layering. The nests usually have a gray color to them. They often endure the harsh winters of the north and you can be surprised to see how many were close at hand over the road ways but which only become visible when the leaves fall. The Bullock's race tends to build a less pendulant cup, and at times it is merely a small shallow cup in a tree crotch made of grasses and plant fiber.

Although the majority of the birds leave the country for the winter a number remain behind at winter feeding stations or in orchards. They feed on fruit at this time, and will come readily to oranges cut in half and placed out in the trees. When times get hard they will take seeds. It is still exciting when a race from the opposite coast shows up "out of range," though they are now one species.

Nests of this species take the form of a pendant, constructed of grass and other fibrous plant material which is decorated with plant down and spiders webs to give them a gray color (above). They are usually placed in a shady situation and are suspended by two handles.

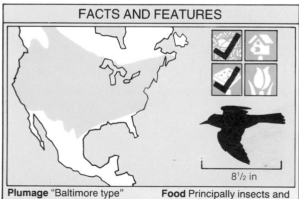

Although mainly a summer resident, a few overwinter. During this period, when their preferred food is scarce, they will venture to the ground in search of seeds. This bird (above), however, is "anting," a phenomenon which involves enticing ants to spray their plumage with formic acid to help remove parasites.

FACTS AND FEATURES

Plumage "Baltimore type" with black hood and brilliant orange body. "Bullock's type": black crown, black line through eye, and black on throat. White wing patch.
Habitat Open woodlands, river forests, shade trees in parks, yards, gardens and orchards.

Food Principally insects and spiders with some fruits and seeds. Fruit in winter.
Nest Pendulant, very well made "pouch" of grasses and plant fibers. Very resilient but will not be used again.

8 1/2 in

147

ORCHARD ORIOLE *Icterus spurius*

THIS SLIM, SWEET SINGING oriole has a rather wide summer range. Throughout the northeast into central Vermont, west through the Dakotas and south throughout most of Texas and to central Florida.

The adult male is a beautiful deep chestnut with a black hood that extends down the back and onto the throat. The wings and tail are jet black. This plumage is not acquired until the second year. In the first year the male is basically the same color as the female, a yellowish green with faint wing bars. However, the first year male has darker wings, streaking on the back and black around the base of the bill and upper breast.

As the name implies it is a bird of city steets, orchards, parklands and gardens. It also enjoys the open spaces of farmland and cool riverine forests.

It is in these shaded trees that the small pendulant nest is built. Not nearly as pendulant as most of the other orioles, it is more cup-like and suspended from a crotch of an outer limb. Made almost entirely of grasses and plant, it is diagnostic that the grasses used are invariably dry grasses. Hence the nest has a dull yellow color to it and can often be located with ease in the green outer leaves of the nesting tree.

In rare instances they have been known to circumvent making their own nest and use the old nests of the northern oriole that have weathered the winter! Evidently when the females were first seen they were termed the "spurious" Baltimore oriole (then the name of northern) as they look like a hybrid form. And it is just possible that the bird was seen using an old Baltimore nest. Often it is a shade tree in the yard or a fruit tree that these birds choose to nest in.

A small orchard or larger fruiting trees in the garden could act as an attraction. If the birds are actively using your grounds with the male singing daily, an onion basket of dried grasses (that are still pliant) and straw fibers would certainly be used for obtaining nesting material. The species migrates completely out of the country for the winter so that feeding trays can not be used to attract them.

FACTS AND FEATURES

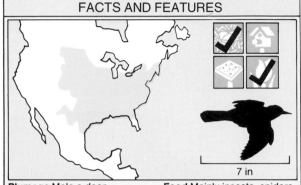

Plumage Male a deep chestnut with black hood extending down back and breast. Black wings and tail. First year male yellow with black mask. Female yellow with gray wings.
Habitat Shade trees, orchards, parks, river forests, open woodland.

Food Mainly insects, spiders and other invertebrates. Some berries and seeds taken.
Nest A cup suspended in fork of outer tree limb. Of dried grasses and plant fibers.

7 in

The male's black and chestnut plumage separates it from the similar, more orange colored northern oriole. Similarly, the lack of orange in the breast of the female separates it from this species. The song is formed of melodious, fluty whistles with a slurred ending.

PURPLE FINCH *Carpodacus purpureus*

THE PURPLE FINCH IS A PERMANENT resident of the west coast population. The contact zone for connection with the eastern population is the summer breeding grounds that stretch across Canada. In the east the resident population runs from Maine south to Maryland and west through the Great Lakes area. During the winter, birds from the summering grounds move south as far as northern Florida and central Texas.

This bird is the "country relative" and lookalike of the house finch, although during the winter months it too will take up residence at the feeding station.

As this bird is not purple it could have been more aptly called the raspberry finch or wine colored finch! A raspberry or rose red color washes the entire body of the male, not concentrated in areas that we see in the often confused house finch. Both the head and bill are large, and most of the time the crown looks like a slight raising to the feathers. A dark brown patch runs through the eye. The female is bulky, large headed with a distinct brown ear patch offset by white lines above the eye and on the lower cheek.

They favor coniferous woods, mixed woodlands, oak forested canyons, mountain slopes, as well as orchards, gardens and parkland. For the most part of the year they wander about in groups and settle down only during the breeding season. The characteristic *tic* note as they pass over at times is the only indication that they are in the area.

The nest is a tight cup of grasses and plant fibers along with some bark strips. If cedars are nearby they will use the fibrous bark for much of the nests outside. The cup is lined with fine grass and hair.

Although mainly a seed eater, during the periods of raising young it will also feed on insect matter. When the nesting period is over they wander in erratic directions and numbers. When visiting the feeder site they are particularly attracted to sunflower and thistle seeds, and will spend whole days feeding at the tray. Then, true to their unpredictable nature, they will be gone perhaps not to return for the winter or to return daily for a time.

FACTS AND FEATURES

6 in

Plumage Male: washed with rose red, streaked on back; grayish underbelly; brown ear patch. Female: brownish streaked flanks; white above and below ear patch.
Habitat Coniferous woodlands, mixed woodlands, oak woodlands, riverine forest, parks, gardens.

Food Principally seeds and fruit; some insects taken. Sunflower and thistle seed at feeders.
Nest Shallow cup of twigs, rootlets, grasses and bark strips usualy in a conifer.

Reddish, not purple, plumage in the male extends over most of the body. The brownish, heavily streaked female is very similar to Cassin's finch, but note the stubbier bill and darker head producing a clearer, whitish line behind the eye, which also separates it from the house finch.

♂

HOUSE FINCH *Carpodacus mexicanus*

THE HOUSE FINCH is the bubbling songster of the backyard and courtyard. A permanent population is found all along the west coast and east to central Texas, Colorado, mid-Wyoming and Idaho. Introduced in the early 1940s to the east coast, the population has made a dramatic explosion in the last 25 years. They are found from the Maine border through the Great Lakes states and south Georgia and Mississippi. Small winter groups move into northern Florida and the Gulf Coast area, and no doubt they will soon establish a permanent residence.

The male is garbed in brown, with streaks on the belly and flanks and rich rosy red (which tends to be orange in western populations) on the forehead, breast and rump. The female is sparrow like with her soft brown coloring and all over streaking.

This abundant species favors weedy areas, brushy hillsides and arid zones in the west. Farmlands and grassland edges are other favorite spots and they seem to do best when living alongside human habitation. Some populations spend their entire lives in one neighborhood, wandering from feeder to feeder and nesting in building overhangs in the summer.

The nest is a large mass of materials, such as plant fiber, twigs and debris, formed into a cup. The inside is lined with fine grasses. The nest may be placed in a decorative evergreen, often right next to the house. Or these adaptable birds may choose an old birdhouse, cavities in trees, building ledges, or abandoned woodpecker holes. One way to attract nesters is to affix an old strawberry box under an overhang—a prized nesting site for this backyard bird.

A large variety of seeds, berries, fruits and insects make up their diet. At the feeding station sunflower seeds are their main target. But peanut butter with seeds is readily taken, as will be fine cracked corn, millet, peanut hearts and thistle seeds. If you ensure a sufficient supply of water, all their needs for backyard residence will be catered for. Their beautiful song will reward your efforts.

FACTS AND FEATURES

6 in

Plumage Male: rosy red to orange on forehead, throat, chest and rump. Brown and streaked over rest of body. Female: all brown and streaked. Very sparrow like.
Habitat Around habitation, backyards, parks, gardens, weedy areas, brushy hillsides, wooded canyons.

Food Seeds and fruits with some insects during nesting. Sunflower seeds are a favorite.
Nest Bulky cup with grass, fibers, bark strips usually placed in a conifer or ornamental shrub.

Smaller and with a more stubby bill than Cassin's or purple finch, the male's brown cap, red forehead, rump and breast, and buffish brown streaks on sides and belly are diagnostic. The female and juveniles are streaked brown and lack any eye stripe or dark mustache.

♀

♂

PINE SISKIN *Carduelis pinus*

A small streaked finch with thin bill and well notched tail—the sexes are similar. In flight, the yellow in the wings and at the base of the tail shows clearly. They are usually seen in small flocks often with goldfinches in winter. The call is a wheezy t wee-ee.

A SLEEK BIRD OF THE coniferous and nearby mixed woodlands of the northeast and west. Their permanent range extends from Maine and northern New York through the Great Lakes area west into central Canada, then the entire area from the rockies westwards. In the arid region of this vast area they are winter visitors.

Male and female are similar. Small billed, heavily streaked with brown on the white underparts and brown back. On the wing and tail there are flash patches of yellow. As with others in the group, such as the goldfinch, the flight is roller coaster in fashion.

They are highly gregarious birds and often move in very large flocks. Being residents of northern areas they are not very often in contact with people, but they are nonetheless, a most confiding species.

The nest in the coniferous belt and the cup of twigs, mosses, bark strips and lichens straddles the branch of a conifer. In years of mass influxes from the north they will often nest far south of the normal range. Such out of range nestings have occurred into Georgia.

At feeders they will often land upon a person bringing out the seeds in anticipation of the feast. But their favorite site is the thistle seed feeder where they take turns on the peg perches probing in for seeds. Though other seeds are taken it is this source that is of highest interest. Indeed the derivation of the generic name of Carduelis finds its roots meaning "thistle eater." If one is not careful with their feeding regime they will stay on at a site well into late spring, far beyond normal migration time, but then nesting impulses will head them north.

A thistle patch in a garden plot can be a joy for attracting this species and goldfinch. They cling monkey-fashion to the pendulant, seed bearing heads as they extract the tiny black seeds. Water should also be supplied and bathing will often occur even in very cold weather.

FACTS AND FEATURES

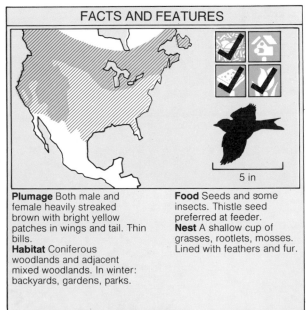

5 in

Plumage Both male and female heavily streaked brown with bright yellow patches in wings and tail. Thin bills.

Habitat Coniferous woodlands and adjacent mixed woodlands. In winter: backyards, gardens, parks.

Food Seeds and some insects. Thistle seed preferred at feeder.

Nest A shallow cup of grasses, rootlets, mosses. Lined with feathers and fur.

COMMON REDPOLL *Carduelis flammea*

♂

♀

This is a small, dumpy finch with yellowish bill, red forehead, black chin, short tail and two buffish white wing bars. The male has a pink rump and breast. The call, from a perch, is a tsoeet, *while in flight it a trilling* tchee tchee tchee.

A BIRD OF NORTHERN CANADA and Alaska, the winter range is basically south to New England, the Great Lakes region, the Dakotas and Montana. South of that line is only visited in major irruption years. This timing is unpredictable and is dependent on food in the north.

A tiny, plump bird of the extremes of the north. The breeding territory is the shrub pockets of the tundra within the arctic circle and the limit of treeline.

Its arrival within the contiguous United States is sporadic. Some years very few birds are seen, in other years flocks in the thousands may visit your backyard.

These hardy birds can fend in the severest weather. The male is marked by a rosy bloom to the breast and a small red cap that gives them their common name. The sides and flanks are streaked. The back is brown and the short tail ends in a deep notch.

The nest is placed in the base of shrubs or tucked into the tundra mat. It is a well made cup of willow fibers and grasses and lined with caribou hair or feathers of the ptarmigan. Within the tree limit zone it may be placed well up in a conifer.

Seeds dominate their diet and they take insects when available. On wintering grounds, seeds are all that is taken. As with their close relatives the goldfinch and the siskin, thistle seed is preferred at the feeder. But oil-seed sunflowers also command a great deal of attention. They shuffle about, feathers fluffed out, sitting close to the ground in severe winter storms. Coming from isolated areas of the north their contact with people is very limited and, therefore, they are most confiding. During winter

visitations catkin-bearing trees such as alder and birch are well worked. Groves of these trees will hold flocks for days. Any garden tree with catkins or seeds will surely be attractive to this species. With the warming of early spring the flocks whisk northward to return at some unknown time.

Brush piles of evergreen material are welcome night roosting areas as well as escape areas from predators.

FACTS AND FEATURES

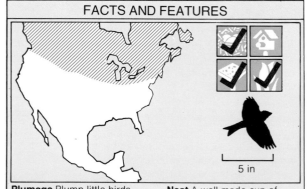

5 in

Plumage Plump little birds, with tiny bills. Rose breast and red cap. Streaked brown back and flanks.
Habitat Open tundra thickets, adjacent conifer woodlands of the far north. Thickets and feeders during the winter.
Food Mainly seeds and fruits but insects taken to feed young.

Nest A well made cup of grasses and plant fibers. Lined with hair and feathers. On ground, in low shrub or at time in conifer well above ground. Prefers willow thickets.

AMERICAN GOLDFINCH *Carduelis tristis*

THIS BRILLIANT LITTLE BIRD IS a permanent resident throughout the United States. It summers in southern Canada, Montana, the Dakotas and the Great Lakes area. If mild winters persist the population is less likely to head further south. The post breeding movement shifts a large population into strictly wintering areas south of their permanent range. From Florida through the Gulf Coast and on through Texas, New Mexico and Arizona the birds put in their only appearance for the year.

Known by many as the "wild canary" this species is highly gregarious, and loose flocks drop down to feed in weedy fields or to feeders bringing a swirl of color and high pitched *su--wee* notes to brighten a day. The male is a brilliant yellow in breeding plumage with a black cap on the forepart on the head, a bright orange bill, and jet black wings and tail. The female is an olive-backed bird with yellow underparts. In fall, the plumage of both birds takes on a drab olive color with the male having darker wings. In any plumage, when viewed from the back, a black and white zebra pattern is noticeable.

Being so widespread, a variety of habitats are frequented. Open woodlands, riverine woods, farm fields, prairies, parks, gardens, are all sure to be visited. Being dependent on seeds for most of its diet, territories are set up in fields rich in weed seeds. However, their territories may be very small and often several pairs will have to share the same locality.

They are notoriously late nesters, waiting for thistle heads to develop their "downy" seeds late into the summer. These seeds are used to line the tight cup which is made from grasses, bark strips, plant fibers and cobwebs. The nest is placed in a supporting crotch or shrubby tree. The young will be fed insect larvae and other invertebrate forms in addition to grass and other small seeds.

Once nesting is over and they begin to wander about in loose bands, feeding trays will be visited. Without question the most attractive item is thistle seeds. These can be scattered or, for most efficient use, placed in a thistle feeder designed specifically for goldfinch and other small finches. Sunflower plantings along with thistles in a garden plot is another sure way to attract groups of these birds. They live well with human habitation and often appear unafraid of nearby people.

FACTS AND FEATURES

Plumage Male: brilliant yellow with black cap, wings and tail. Orange bill. Female: olive drab above, yellowish below.
Habitat Open fields, weedy areas, roadsides, farmlands, gardens, secondary growth areas.

Food Insects taken during nesting, but principally seeds. Especially thistle and sunflower.
Nest A beautiful cup of grasses and plant fibers in shrub fork. Always lined with thistle "down."

5 in

Smaller than the similarly marked evening grosbeak the American goldfinch has a much stubbier bill. The male's bright summer plumage is lost in the winter when he becomes brownish gray above and loses the black on the crown. Females are much duller than males, and lack the black cap and the yellow on the shoulder.

♂

EVENING GROSBEAK *Coccothraustes vespertinus*

A BIRD OF THE NORTHERN and western coniferous forests of Canada and the west. In the east, the only permanent range is in northern New England and the Great Lakes region. The western population follow the mountains through to Washington and Oregon and into central California, Arizona and New Mexico. Depending on the mast (winter cone and berry crop) flocks of these birds move south in the winter. During this time they may invade as far south as Georgia, Texas and Louisiana.

They build their bulky twig nest in a conifer and line it with hair or feathers and, at times, mosses.

When the cry of *'there are parrots at my feeder'* comes ,it

Often seen in flocks, the yellow plumage combined with the heavy, yellowish white, conical bill distinguish the evening grosbeak. The grayer female has a white tip to the tail and two white patches in the wing. Sunflower seeds at the feeding station will attract it.

♂

is certain to be this species. The bright colors and very large bill impart the tropical aspect.

The male is a bulky bird with bright yellow back and underparts. The neck and throat is a smoky gray with a black cap. Over the eye is a brilliant yellow line. White primaries form the lower back and are seen as wing patches in flight. The female is a warm buff brown with gray on its back and head. The white in the wings shows in her also. Both have pale bills tough enough to crack cherry pits.

Outside of the coniferous zone they spread into a great variety of habitats. Mixed woodlands, parks, gardens, and certainly backyard feeding stations.

In the crisp air of the fall the penetrating *peeer* notes can be heard as flocks of birds pass overhead. Depending on the food supply of seeds and berries they will make irregular influxes into the southern areas. Some years, when cones are abundant, hardly any will show at feeders. Other years, flocks will remain all winter at one feeding station. Here, they put on a show of how sunflower seeds should be husked. They sit by the hour on the tray until not one is left to eat. Then they retire to a nearby tree and wait for more to be put out.

Planting stands of sunflower in a garden patch will certainly attract them. Or simply snip off the seed heads and lay them out on the tray. These birds will not hesitate to pick their own seeds. Their color, abundance (in some years) and diligence at the feeder make them one of the best known and most looked for species at the winter feeding sites.

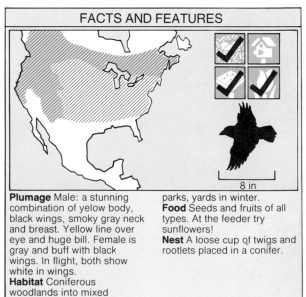

FACTS AND FEATURES

8 in

Plumage Male: a stunning combination of yelow body, black wings, smoky gray neck and breast. Yellow line over eye and huge bill. Female is gray and buff with black wings. In flight, both show white in wings.
Habitat Coniferous woodlands into mixed woodlands and gardens, parks, yards in winter.
Food Seeds and fruits of all types. At the feeder try sunflowers!
Nest A loose cup of twigs and rootlets placed in a conifer.

RED CROSSBILL *Loxia curvirostra*

THE RANGE OF THIS BIRD extends from the coniferous forests of Canada, through mountains of the western United States and on into the mountains of Mexico.

This raspberry red bird has dark wings and a most unusual bill that is crossed at the tips. The females are yellowish green with dark wings and have a conspicuous yellow rump. They are often very tame and you can approach to within arms length.

Outside the mountain areas most people know this species as a bird of the winter feeder. They come down from the north in rather irregular patterns with years of poor mast (seed and cone crop) in the north being the main force for these irruptions. A few pass through every year, but in some years the incursions see the birds everywhere. They are attracted to conifers and in such regions can often be seen feeding on gravel or salt alongside the road. In the clear winter air, the loud *chiff chiff* of flocks flying overhead or feeding atop a conifer is usually the first indication that they are present. Allowing a close approach one can literally walk past them without realizing they are there.

Plantings of conifers such as red, black or white pines along with spruces are sure to attract birds during winter movements. They will come readily to a feeding station if sunflower seeds or thistle seeds are available. These can be put out on a feeding tray or scattered on the ground. The thistle seeds, being small are best placed in a thistle feeder which is available commercially. With the high cost of thistle seed in mind, such a feeder will allow the most economical dispensing of seed. Once a feeding site is selected by the crossbills, they usually take up residence for the winter. In cases of large incursions from the north they have been known to nest as far south as Georgia. Again, conifers are the preferred site, but in some instances they have even nested in the ivy covering walls.

FACTS AND FEATURES

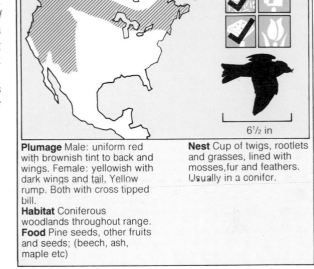

6½ in

Plumage Male: uniform red with brownish tint to back and wings. Female: yellowish with dark wings and tail, Yellow rump. Both with cross tipped bill.
Habitat Coniferous woodlands throughout range.
Food Pine seeds, other fruits and seeds; (beech, ash, maple etc)

Nest Cup of twigs, rootlets and grasses, lined with mosses, fur and feathers. Usually in a conifer.

♀

♂

The large head and crossed bill are the distinguishing features. The bill may be crossed either way and allows the bird to open pine cones to extract the seed inside. Juveniles do not develop the crossed mandibles until they have left the nest. The lack of wing bars separates it from the white-winged crossbill.

USEFUL ADDRESSES

Local bird clubs, Audubon groups, or ornithological societies are to be found in nearly every state and Canadian province, especially in the larger cities. These clubs hold meetings, lectures and field trips for the general public. Many groups publish newsletters and journals.

Meetings occasionally include motion pictures or slides of birds as well as other wildlife films and lectures. To locate these and other nature societies consult the Conservation Directory of the National Wildlife Federation, your state conservation department, or the library or newspaper of your home town.

UNITED STATES OF AMERICA

American Birding Association
P.O. Box 4335
Austin
Texas 78765

American Ornithologists Union
Museum of Natural History
Smithsonian Institution
Washington
DC 20560

National Audubon Society
950 Third Avenue
New York
NY 10022

Flora & Fauna Preservation Society Inc.
P.O. Box 1108
Boston
MA 02130

CANADA

Canada Nature Federation
75 Albert Street
Ottawa K1P 6G1

FURTHER READING

The Audubon Society Master Guide To Birding 1983
J. Farrand
(3 vols.)

The Birds Of Canada
W.E. Godfrey

Field Guide To The Birds Of North America
National Geographical Society

A Field Guide To The Birds East Of The Rockies
Peterson Field Guide Series 1
(4th ed. revised 1984)

A Field Guide To Western Birds
Peterson Field Guide Series 2

A Field Guide To Texas And Adjacent States
Peterson Field Guide Series 13

INDEX

Numbers in bold type indicate the main entry for each species of bird. Numbers in italic type indicate references to illustrations.

Picture Credits

Key: t=top; b=bottom; r=right; l=left; i=inset.

6/7 Karen Bussolini. *7* Eric Crichton. *9* Eric Crichton. *10/11* Eric Hosking. *11* Frank Lane. *12(b)* Karen Bussolini. *12(t)* Eric Crichton. *12/13* Eric Crichton. *13* Frank Lane. *14(b)* Lennart Norström. *14(t)* Eric Crichton. *14/15* Karen Bussolini. *16(b)* Frank Lane. *16(t)* Eric Crichton. *17* David Hosking. *30* Nick Clark. *31* Trevor Wood. *31(i)* Trevor Wood. *32/33* Trevor Wood. *34* Eric & David Hosking. *40* Frank Lane. *43(b)* Eric & David Hosking. *43(tl)* Eric Hosking. *43(tr)* Frank Lane. *46(bl)* Frank Lane. *46(br)* Frank Lane. *47* Frank Lane.

Other pictures supplied by Eric & David Hosking, Leonard Lee Rue, L. West, B. R. Young and Ron Austing.